THE BOOK I READ

Inspiring Stories

created by

*Lynda Sunshine West and
Sally Larkin Green*

ACTION TAKERS
—— PUBLISHING ——
WE TAKE ACTION SO YOU DON'T HAVE TO

ActionTakersPublishing™
SanDiego, California

Action Takers Publishing™
www.actiontakerspublishing.com

ebook ISBN: 978-1-956665-03-1
Paperback ISBN: 978-1-956665-04-8

100% of the net proceeds of the sales of this book will be donated to a 501(c)(3) nonprofit charity.

Cover Design by Sam Art Studio
Printed in the United States of America

TABLE OF CONTENTS

"See yourself through the eyes of others,
for others see the real you."
~*Lynda Sunshine West*

A SUNNY NOTE FROM LYNDA SUNSHINE WEST AND SALLY LARKIN GREEN

Warning!! This book will positively impact your life.

How this book was born …

Sometimes an idea hits you over the head and you "go with it." Other times, you slough it off and move on with your day.

Lynda Sunshine's husband, who is a musician, was watching a YouTube video of a band from the 1970s called The Talking Heads. The song he was listening to is called "The Book I Read." As they watched the goofy video while laughing hysterically, Scott said something that Lynda Sunshine heard loud and clear. He said, "You should do a collaboration book called *The Book I Read*." They both laughed, then Lynda Sunshine said, "That's a great idea." So here we are today, sharing this book that sparked from a small idea.

We immediately (we are action takers, after all) went to the drawing board and started thinking of ways to make this into a really cool book. We asked each other if there was a particular book that changed our life. Both of us, without hesitation, came up with the number one book that was transformational. It was through this conversation that we realized books have a way of changing people's lives if they are open to seeing the possibilities.

The idea came to us that we could share stories from 50 incredible women and men from all over the world that we've met during our journeys. In *The Book I Read*, these authors talk about the transformation they have experienced that started with reading one book. Because our authors are from all over the world, you may notice some words spelled (or spelt) differently than you're used to. We kept the spellings from their country to retain the integrity of each author's heritage.

From a math textbook to a child's Dr. Seuss book to the Bible to some of the self-help standards you're expecting, you may be surprised to read how their lives were transformed. No matter the book, the transformations are real.

You have undoubtedly read a book or two (maybe more) at some point in your life. Some of the books you've read have made a big difference and you were impacted to the point of transformation. That's what this book is all about. This is NOT a book report. This is NOT a book review. This is all about transformation.

"Books for me have always been a way to escape. I now consider reading a good book a sacred indulgence, time alone to be anyplace I choose. It is my absolute favorite way to spend time. What I know for sure is that reading opens you up."
~Oprah Winfrey

You're about to embark on a journey. Everyone has a story to tell, a story to share. While you read this book, think about your own journey … What's your story? What book has transformed your life? Then share that book and this book with a friend.

At Action Takers Publishing, our mission is to empower 5,000,000 women and men to share their stories with the world to make a greater impact on the planet. We do this because we realize the power of sharing your story and how it can transform somebody else's life. We definitely need more positivity in this world and this is our way of doing that.

When you're ready to make a greater impact on the planet, we're here. Just reach out to us at www.ActionTakersPublishing.com.

With gratitude,

Lynda Sunshine West and Sally Larkin Green

CHAPTER 1

FEAR-FULL TO FEAR-LESS

by Lynda Sunshine West
Founder & CEO, Action Takers Publishing
www.ActionTakersPublishing.com

As I sat down to write this chapter, I started experiencing flashbacks back to a time when things weren't so good. As a matter of fact, my life was so dark that I literally felt like I was walking around in a dark cloud, you know, like that Charlie Brown character, Pig Pen, whose whole like is engulfed in dust following him everywhere he goes.

What's crazy is as I was in that darkness, filled with anger, disgust, hate, anguish, judgment, anxiety, fear, and a whole bunch of other negative emotions, I didn't know it was bad. It was all I knew.

When you grow up in a toxic environment, you think that's just how life is. "Anyone who says they're happy is a liar." That was my belief.

I grew up in an extremely volatile, abusive, alcoholic household. I hated (down to my core) my dad. All I saw when I looked at his deeply furrowed brow was a MONSTER. Literally, I saw a monster.

My hate and disdain for him lasted until several years after he passed away. Even worse? I carried that loathing and disgust around for 51 years.

It was a Thursday night. Mom and dad walked into the hospital because dad was having chest pains. He had had a pacemaker inserted about three years earlier, after having had a double bypass surgery at the age of 35 and a triple bypass several years later. He had also had colon cancer, and prostate cancer twice, and some other medical issues. I used to call him the Energizer Bunny because every five years he had a major surgery and kept on ticking.

Mom and dad didn't tell us he was checked into the hospital. THIS WAS ROUTINE!

Friday morning I received a phone call from mom. "Dad is in the hospital and we don't think he's gonna make it."

After 45 years of chaos and turmoil, I had zero emotions connected to her words.

I told my husband (who absolutely adored my dad) and we drove to the hospital.

When we arrived, we found out that dad had had "86 heart attacks since last night." His pacemaker was keeping him alive.

86 HEART ATTACKS

After 55 years of marriage, mom was frozen in fear, but not for the reason you might be thinking.

"Mom, you gotta tell the doctor to turn off his pacemaker. He's not coming back," I said.

"I can't do it. You do it."

Everyone was there. My siblings, the grandkids, dad's friend from AA. We all stood there watching dad's death unfold.

No matter how much of a monster he was, I didn't like seeing him have so many heart attacks. It was time to let him go.

I went to the nurse's station and told them to unplug dad's pacemaker.

As we stood there against the wall in complete silence (nowhere near his hospital bed), the doctor walked into the room and turned off his pacemaker.

My husband and I were standing right next to mom.

The first words out of mom's mouth after dad took his last breath shook me to my core. I had no idea how bad it had been for mom those 55 years. I mean, I witnessed it, but she never said anything. She stifled her voice for decades.

TRIGGER WARNING!

The doctor pronounced him dead. "THANK GOD THE BASTARD IS DEAD." Mom said those words under her breath and loud enough for me and Scott to hear.

Finally, after 55 years, she could breathe a sigh of relief.

Remember when I said mom couldn't tell the doctor to turn off the pacemaker and it wasn't the reason you were thinking? You see, mom lived her life believing that she could never make a right decision. Dad made sure she knew it, too. Dad was a narcissist, a gaslighter. Mom was led to believe she couldn't make a right decision, so she didn't.

Having grown up in that environment, I took on some very similar characteristics as mom. My first marriage was to someone just like dad. I got out of there after two of the longest and darkest years of my life. The best thing about my first marriage is the two incredible humans we made together.

One day I had had enough. Jeanna was 4 weeks old and Timmy was 14 months old. I picked up my purse and threw it over my right shoulder. I then picked up the diaper bag and threw it over my left shoulder. I put Timmy on my right hip and Jeanna in her baby carry case and we literally walked out (I didn't have a car). I was <u>not</u> going to repeat my mom's life. I was 21 years old with two babies. I didn't want them to live the life I lived.

As I look back on that day, I was very smart and brave to walk out. However, I did it because I was scared…. for my life and for my kids' lives.

I spent the next several decades living my life behind fear. Fear controlled me.

Until I was 51 years old, August 2014.

What was different? Well, I ended up hiring a life coach. She helped me open my mind to possibilities, MY possibilities.

January 1, 2015, I woke up and decided to do something different. I had this realization that I had a lot of fears and they were stopping me from those opportunities. So I decided to break through a fear every day that year. And I did.

One of the things that really helped me that year was reading self-help books. I read them, took notes, and "acted on" what I learned.

So many books put me on a course of transformation, but one, in particular, REALLY changed my life.

Actually, it was the first chapter that changed my life. Actually, in reality, it was the TITLE of the first chapter that transformed my life.

"TAKE 100% RESPONSIBILITY FOR YOUR LIFE" is the first principle in Jack Canfield's *The Success Principles*.

I spent so many years holding onto the anger and hate I had for my dad that I blamed him for mostly everything. I blamed my mom for staying with him. I blamed employers for jobs I hated. I blamed my ex-husband for my life with him.

This one title in this one chapter empowered me with the ability to accept 100% responsibility for my life.

I grew tremendously from a negative into a positive person. From someone who didn't believe in herself to someone who knows her value. From terrified to terrific. From Fear-Full to Fear-Less.

I LOVE MY LIFE and it all started with me raising my hand to say, "I'm ready to change my life."

LYNDA SUNSHINE WEST

As the Founder and CEO of Action Takers Publishing, Lynda Sunshine West's mission is to empower 5 million women and men to share their stories with the world to make a greater impact on the planet. She is affectionately known as The Queen of Collaboration. Lynda Sunshine is a Book Publisher, Speaker, Multiple Times #1 International Bestselling Author, Executive Film Producer, and a Red Carpet Interviewer. At the age of 5, she ran away and was gone an entire week. She came home riddled with fears that stopped her from living. At age 51, she decided to face one fear every day for an entire year. In doing so, she gained an exorbitant amount of confidence and now uses what she learned to fulfill her mission. Action Takers Publishing's motto is "We take action so you don't have to."

Connect with Lynda Sunshine at
www.ActionTakersPublishing.com

CHAPTER 2

IF MY FRIENDS COULD SEE ME NOW!

by Sally Larkin Green
Creative Director, Action Takers Publishing
www.ActionTakersPublishing.com

When I was asked to write about a book that transformed my life, the answer was easy. I was going to write about *The Master Key System* by Charles Haanel because of the effect the words of this book had on my life. By reading and studying *The Master Key System*, I was able to ease my anxiety and control my thoughts; it helped me reignite my imagination and find peace in being still. I have studied it and taught classes on The Master Key System for over 10 years. Although this book laid the foundation, there is another book that completely changed my life.

The book I am talking about transformed my life not by the words written on the pages, but by the people I met and the shifts I made in my life because of it. The book is called: *1 Habit for Entrepreneurial Success*.

In December of 2019, I decided I wanted to start a new business teaching paint and wine classes. I connected with an organization who would sponsor me. I ordered business cards and started advertising. In January I began contacting senior centers and was able to secure three monthly accounts. I started a Saturday morning coffee and canvas class in my church hall that was well received. Then the pandemic hit in March of 2020. All of my painting classes stopped, and we lost a major client in our small cleaning business. I was devastated.

It was around that time that I woke up one morning, looked in the mirror and realized I was a mess. I knew if I kept letting my thoughts and my life spiral out of control, I would get to the point very soon where I wouldn't be able to climb out of it. I started with the one thing I knew I could control, my food. I got my daughter and husband on board, and we immediately began eating healthier. I started purchasing low fat, reduced calorie items. We cut out sugary treats, snacks, bread, and alcohol. In addition, we began walking every day.

By July, I had lost 30 pounds and was feeling hopeful. I had been Facebook friends with Forbes Riley since 2008 when I saw her on TV on HSN. I had purchased her Spin-Gym, sent her a Facebook friend request with a message telling her how much I loved her product. One night while I was scrolling through Facebook, I saw that Forbes was on live. She was talking about a collaboration book she was working on. She was looking for people to write a chapter in a book called *1 Habit for Entrepreneurial Success*. I laughed and asked myself, "Could I really write a chapter in that book?"

My husband and I have been small business owners for over 25 years. Our business helped pay the bills plus a tiny bit extra. We were making enough to survive, but was that considered successful? Who was I to write a chapter in a book about entrepreneurial success? But on the other hand, the investment was minimal, and I had always wanted to be a writer. I made the decision to do it. That night, without even thinking it through, I pulled out my credit card and registered to write a chapter in the book. Now I had to write my chapter.

I had just finished watching a Hallmark movie where the woman was afraid of heights and the guy wanted to take her on a hot air balloon ride. He convinced her by holding her hand and telling her to do it afraid. I thought that was a great message, so that was what I wrote about. I titled my chapter "Do It Afraid" and submitted it.

The next thing I knew I was in a Facebook group with the other authors. I was connecting with many influential businesspeople and entrepreneurs who were part of the book. I quickly realized I was out of my element, but I was having so much fun, enjoying the conversations, and making new friends with positive, uplifting people.

When the book arrived, I couldn't wait to read the chapters and bios of all the authors I had met. I decided I wanted to start a new business, but I was uncertain what path to take. I could rekindle my art classes online, teach bible studies, or maybe I could help women on their wellness journey. I needed help and a mentor. I knew exactly where to go to find one.

In December of 2020, while in the authors' group, one of the women in the book invited those interested to a woman's networking event on Zoom. Her speaker was an Olympic gold medalist, so I registered for the event and joined her Facebook group. She made a post inside the Facebook group that read, "What would you ask an Olympic gold medalist?" A bunch of questions came to my mind, so I typed them in the comments. I attended the event and met a bunch of new women. It was so much fun. Lynda Sunshine West was the host and she told me about a business mastermind she was leading called "Be Seen, Be Heard, Be Paid." I contacted her and signed up for it. There were five of us and we met weekly beginning in February of 2021.

Lynda Sunshine helped me create a new business, encouraged me to keep going when no one was watching my YouTube interviews, and invited me to be part of the collaboration books she was publishing. She quickly became my mentor and friend. In October of 2021, we partnered together to create Action Takers Publishing specializing in collaboration books.

So here I am full circle. I have gone from writing my first collaboration book to becoming the Creative Director at a publishing company in less than 2 years. Excuse me as I break out in song: "What a setup, holy cow. They'd never believe it if my friends could see me now."

SALLY LARKIN GREEN

Sally Larkin Green lives in Connecticut. She and her husband have been small business owners for over 25 years. Sally is an acrylic and watercolor artist, speaker, and a self-care rockstar. She is a multiple time international #1 bestselling author. She enjoys her 3 cats, especially her 23-pound Maine coon cat named Hank who loves to attend Zoom calls with her.

Sally is the Creative Director at Action Takers Publishing specializing in themed collaboration books. Their mission is to empower 5 million women and men to share their story with the world to make a greater impact on the planet.

Sally is also a self-care coach and mentor helping women begin and continue their self-care journey both physically and spiritually. Sally has written two bible studies, leads masterminds, and teaches The Master Key System principles.

You can connect with Sally at www.ActionTakersPublishing.com.

CHAPTER 3

WHO'S IN MY ROOM?

by Alice Pallum
Founder, AMP Business Coaching & Consulting
www.ampbusinesscoaching.com

It was and is a journey; the results are amazing!

Approximately eight years ago I read *Who's in Your Room* by Ivan R. Misner, Ph.D., Stewart Emery L.H.D., and Rick Sapio.

"Imagine you live in one room, with one door?"

And I did. This really spoke to me.

Who would I let in?

Who would I move out?

This book lays out a great process for this work.

And it starts with me. What are my values? What is important to me? What is deplorable to me?

So I did the work, made the list.

Then I looked at how these related to the pieces of my life.

This book was actually introduced to me by way of my membership in BNI (Business Network International). It is a great resource for BNI members and especially individuals who operate as the Membership Committee for a chapter. But it also applies to your business and your life.

The first leg of the journey was easiest. How to apply this to my BNI chapter. As we looked at this as a chapter, what were the values of the chapter? What would make us successful? As we evaluated the chapter, past and present, it was clear how different people and personalities could affect the entire group. This was a slow, and sometimes difficult, process to implement, but it was worthwhile.

Looking at the successful characteristic of a business and BNI member was clear. You could see the effects on the entire group as members came and went. It created an "avatar" of the members who would be successful in the group.

The second leg of the journey–applying this to my business. Who did I want to do business with? Who did I want to let into this room?

Which clients were helping me grow in my business? Which clients were a drain on my business?

This was a very important question.

I applied the same process. What were my values? What were my goals? As I took stock–I could see the trends. The clients who were enthusiastic. The clients who were coachable and open to change. These were the clients I needed in my room.

The opposite was true as well. Clients who were not coachable and not open to making changes were a drain on my business and me.

I started by being more selective about who I was letting into this room. I trained my "Doorman" to say no.

Then I needed to take a look at who and what was already in this room.

This is where the "Art of Benign Neglect" was very useful. It helps move the people and things, that are not a fit for your room, further to the back, where there is less time and focus.

The results have been fantastic!

Business is growing, more fulfilling, and less stressful.

These clients refer more clients like themselves.

This also helped me identify who is a good fit as a collaboration partner. This has also had a great effect. I have three different collaborations going and they are all adding to the business.

The last leg of the journey–applying this to my life–was the hardest. Who did I want to let into this room?

I was at a point in life where I had let a lot of people "into my room" and they were not all a good fit.

As I took a look, I observed several things. After interacting with several people in my room–I had a very negative outlook. Was this interaction in my best interest?

Others were leaving me with a defeated attitude. Were these interactions in my best interest?

Of course the tough answer was no!

There were others that left me upbeat and positive–even empowered. Were these interactions in my best interest–yes!

So, this helped me with the very difficult process of sorting those interactions.

This was more difficult than applying this thought process to my clients. Some of these people had been in my room for years.

How do I go about this sorting process?

And this circled back to my values. Who or what aligned with them and who/what did not.

I also consulted with some of my close friends.

"The Art of Benign Neglect" applied here as well. The beauty of this is that it is benign! And it starts to happen unconsciously. You start to not respond to things as quickly or you don't call as often.

Has this been easy? No.

Has it been the right thing to do? Yes!

As I said–it has been a journey.

I am happy to share that it has been well worth the journey!

ALICE PALLUM

Alice Pallum is an Award-Winning #1 International Bestselling Author, Accountability Ninja, Goal Setting Master, Harley Rider, and Cool Aunt. She is also the founder of AMP Enterprises, LTD. She has been an entrepreneur for 18 years and she uses this experience combined with her 17 years at American Express to bring a unique combination of skills and experience to her clients.

Alice brings order to chaos and peace to the stress of the seemingly never-ending grind of keeping a business on track and thriving. One of Alice's key skills is the ability to look at the big picture and then dive down into the details. She sees how the pieces fit together. Alice works with business owners and entrepreneurs on an individual, group, and workshop basis. She works in the areas of planning, accountability and root cause identification and solutions. She walks with you through the journey to success. Alice loves learning and is always in search of new experiences and opportunities. Alice is also a member of the Board of Directors of Firefighters with PTSD as the business coach. On a personal note–Alice is a stroke survivor and thriver.

Connect with Alice at www.AMPBusinessCoaching.com.

CHAPTER 4

SURRENDERING TO THE MAGIC

by Annie Rettic
Gratitude Rippler, Annie Rettic Music
https://www.annierettic.com

In 2017, I read a book that changed my life two years later. The book, which was recommended to me by a fellow speaker in a mastermind, was *The Surrender Experiment* by Michael A. Singer. The author describes how beginning a meditation practice to quell his ego led to establishing a Temple, a building company, and finally a groundbreaking medical software company! By letting go of his own agenda for his life, and trusting that Spirit knew a better path he couldn't even imagine, he simply surrendered to it, acting intuitively on what appeared in front of him.

I was fascinated by his amazing life journey, especially how everything he needed appeared miraculously at the right moment. *Trust!* I recalled a time long ago in my own life, when I was expecting my first child. Believing childbirth to be a natural process that modern medicine had altered, I didn't want to have my baby in a hospital. I wanted a "home birth"–even though I didn't have a home! I was on a spiritual path (in a Hippy way), so I simply let go of the need to know HOW it would come to pass.

And magically, serendipitously, everything fell into place. The right doctor and the place where she was born appeared when I needed them to. Reading Michael's book brought all the details and feeling of that time flooding back to me.

Flash forward two years to April 2019. My life was in turmoil. There was a huge boulder from my past that was blocking me from moving forward, and I knew what I had to do. It was necessary to take a road trip from California to Michigan to remove it.

The time had come to end my divorce, which had dragged on for 15 years.

When we ended our marriage, my husband and I split everything down the middle-except for one rather large asset. We owned a lot on a harbor in Michigan's Upper Peninsula. Because it was trapezoid shaped with only 150 ft. of road frontage, the County wouldn't let us split it. For 15 years we'd been like a pair of albatrosses with our legs tied together, going around in circles. In order to move forward financially and emotionally, I needed this final chain to be cut.

The previous summer, my ex-husband and I had discussed putting a small portable cabin on the property, to make it more attractive to buyers. We agreed that a 12'x16' cabin was the perfect size, and we agreed to split the $7,000 cost. That was as far as we got before I returned to California.

Now my life was unraveling. It was time to act! Flying in wasn't an option; I knew that to achieve our plan, I'd need to stay in Michigan for as long as it took. Luckily our daughter had a home I could stay in.

Since moving to San Diego, I had driven solo between the two states half a dozen times, and I'd always found it incredibly stressful. This time was even more so for two reasons: I was giving up my apartment and moving my belongings into a storage unit, and I had a "deadline" to arrive by mid-April if I wanted us to check on the property together. I began the drive a week behind "schedule," with a double dose of my usual anxiety.

But somewhere in Arizona, everything changed. As I bedded down in my hotel room, I received a phone call from my friend Crystal. "Annie, are you OK? We've been so worried about you with the tornadoes in Texas last week!" I realized that if I'd left when I planned, I might not be alive! I checked the weather in Michigan. If I were arriving, I'd be in the middle of a blizzard! In that moment, I remembered what I already knew, which had been reawakened when I read *The Surrender Experiment*.

Right then, I surrendered! I let go of my own agenda, my need to be on someone else's schedule. I ***trusted*** that the universe's plan was far better than anything I could imagine. A Mantra came to me: *"I'm on God's Time."* I knew that whenever I arrived would be the right time.

The next day as I drove, I repeated my mantra. I actually enjoyed the rest of the trip. When I got there, my ex felt the transformation; no explanation was necessary.

Two days later, on Easter Sunday, we drove the 450 miles to the property. Together, we decided where the cabin would be, and what trees had to come down. We were working together. Magic was happening!

On Monday, led by intuition, we took a drive around the Upper Peninsula. Thirty miles from our property we saw a 12'x16' cabin with a For Sale sign! Miraculous! We got the phone number and called the builder. Imagine our joy when we discovered he wanted $3,500—half of what we'd seen online!

That weekend was the beginning of many magical things occurring that spring.

The builder also cut down the trees and delivered the cabin. In June, when it was happening, the bugs were merciless. Camping wasn't an option. Miraculously, there was a cancellation at a resort 1/4 mile down the road. I got to stay in a beautiful cabin with a stove, shower, lights–and no bugs!

On June 21, I made coffee as I watched the sunrise. Then I walked over to a beautiful sight–our cabin. Trusting and surrendering allowed it to happen in a way I never could have dreamed.

ANNIE RETTIC

A nnie Rettic is a storytelling musician and multi-instrumentalist who empowers, educates, and entertains her audiences with spellbinding stories and heartfelt songs which draw people in so they want to sing along. They leave uplifted, with real-world take-aways they can use every day.

Annie's mission is to create a wave of Forgiveness and Gratitude that will help wash away current anger and despair. She is currently recording a series of interviews: *"Stories of Forgiveness and Gratitude."*

Annie Rettic is a lifelong musician. She graduated from Northwestern University in Evanston, Illinois, with a Bachelor's degree in Vocal Performance. One day she realized, *"I want to write my own songs and bare my soul like Joni Mitchell!"* She built a Mountain Dulcimer, did a long deep dive into Folk, Bluegrass and Celtic music, and found her own unique style.

Annie now delivers Keynote Concerts which engage and enchant her audiences with her songs and stories.

Her favorite talk is "*It's Never Too Late to Follow Your Dream.*" She shares her own journey of failure and struggle, and how it led her to the daily practice of Gratitude and the path of Forgiveness which continues to illuminate and transform her life into one she never dreamed was possible.

In 2018, Annie released her 7th CD and first solo recording, *Heartstrings*, containing the songs she performs during her Keynote Concerts.

Connect with Annie here: https://www.annierettic.com

CHAPTER 5

FINDING FREEDOM

by Asma Yousif
Clarity & Confidence Coach
www.asmayousif.com

The book that changed my life is *The Four Agreements* by Don Miguel Ruiz. Before I read this book, I didn't understand what it meant to be authentic to yourself.

I was at a place in my life where I wasn't feeling authentic. Something inside me was not aligned, but I wasn't clear on what (or whom) I needed to be aligned with, or to. I felt myself just living life and not really living life to its fullest potential! I would go to Barnes and Noble and sit in their New Age aisle just searching for something. Not even aware at that time I was searching for myself. I came across this book called *The Four Agreements*. Of course my mind started to question, "What does that look like? What does it mean to have an agreement with myself?" I was intrigued.

I was not focused on myself. Was trying to please everyone else around me. Saying yes to things I wanted to say no to. Found myself very unhappy on the inside even though I wore a smile on the outside. I thought this was normal and this way of living was the right way. I was always told to please people. Always care about what they have to say. Always care about how they feel. Always try to make others happy and to fit in. And it didn't matter whether I was happy or not. I had to live my life the way others were accepting of me. And that did not sit well with me. I was searching for something outside of myself.

When I picked up this book, it brought me inside of myself. It helped me realize I'm the one that holds the power. I'm the one in control over me and my choices. I'm the one in control of my happiness. Happiness is our birthright. When did I let that be taken away from me? I get to get that back. *The Four Agreements* helped me light the fire inside of me. That was the beginning of my internal light turning on and shining bright!

While reading *The Four Agreements*, there were many life lesson takeaways that I still implement to this day. The biggest one that stood out for me is living my authentic self. And being impeccable with my words. Words can do so much. They could bring someone down or they could bring someone up. So, I live my life saying what I mean and not being afraid to use my words. It's also the way I get to live authentically.

As I continued diving deeper into the book, I started to test it out in my everyday life. I wanted to see if this was a real way of living or if it was all just a bunch of words. This book helped transform my way of thinking and my way of being. It really helps me think about my reality and how I am a source and the creator of my reality. What we think and what we believe we manifest. That is what we are creating. What do I want to create in my life? What kind of things do I want to manifest? Does it all come down to the doing? Or does it boil down to the being? This book helped me realize it is our ways of being that matter the most. Be. Do. Have.

Before I picked up this book, I was really desperate for ways of learning. I wanted to understand different ways of living because I knew we had so much control over our own thoughts and our creation.

I have gone on to buy Don Miguel's other books, *The Four Agreements* companion books, *The Mastery of Love*, *The Circle of Fire*, and *The Fifth Agreement*, as well as *The Voice of Knowledge*. I've become a huge fan of this author and his ways of living. Today I get to live my life in the most authentic ways possible. That doesn't mean I don't continue questioning and being curious. I want to continue evolving in learning and growing. This book opened the door to a new reality for me. It helped me look at things through a different lens. It also helped me shift the way I think about things and pay more attention to the words that come out of my mouth. I was raised to not let words affect me. After reading this book, I realize words do have a huge effect on people. And they had a huge effect on me.

Today I have a contract with myself that I say to myself multiple times a day. It is written on a big white board and placed right next to my seat/desk. I say this contract to remind myself who I truly am! As I step into meetings, situations, or events that have my fears and insecurities rising, I go back to my contract. Then I step into my day authentically, knowing my intentions.

When you pick up a book, what is the thing you're looking forward to learning? What are you wanting to change in your life? Those are some good questions to ask yourself before picking up any book. That is what I was asking myself and the reason for me picking up this book.

It changed my life's path and the direction I was headed. I would say this book saved me from making very bad choices and going down a dark path I knew I wouldn't have been able to get myself out of. I wish for you to be able to find comfort and escape into a book that brings you freedom and internal love. My self-love journey started over 25 years ago. This is a life journey I choose to stay on until the day I die. I am grateful for authors like Don Miguel Ruiz who share their teachings, insights, and spirituality with the world.

Happy reading!

ASMA YOUSIF

Asma Yousif is a Clarity and Confidence Coach and is currently working on her certification in Holistic Body Wellness. She has been involved in personal development for many years and her curiosity with the human brain has enhanced her talents. Asma believes what we tell ourselves represents the life we're living. She supports men and women in their personal and professional lives to reclaim their life which they had been living in avoidance and embark on living a life by design and purpose. We do this by shedding layers and years of pent-up anger, self-sabotage, fear, judgment, comparison, and perfectionism to arise into higher ways of living. Her mission is to heighten millions of beautiful humans across the globe and enhance their pursuit of living with greater purpose, clarity, and passion.

It is important for Asma to help create new pathways of thinking, believing, living, and breaking down generational barriers that weigh us down.

She believes that leaders effectively lead when emotional wellness is achieved.

Connect with Asma here: www.asmayousif.com

CHAPTER 6

FROM FROZEN TO FIERCE

by Becky Mosbrucker
Founder, Forward Safety Training, LLC
www.forwardsafetytraining.com

There have been many things I would have liked to do in my lifetime, but didn't—because I was afraid. I tell myself I have no desire to skydive because I'm afraid of heights. But, would I do it if I wasn't afraid? You bet. Absolutely!

What kind of things would you do if you could do it unafraid? Climb a mountain, go skydiving, snow skiing, drive a motorcycle, go to a concert, ride a horse, go scuba diving, give a speech to a large crowd?

Joyce Meyer's book "Do It Afraid" is the perfect how-to that'll get you started. Ms. Meyer is an accomplished author/minister and has been in ministry for over 40 years. She founded Joyce Meyer Ministries in 1987 as a Christian, non-profit organization that is financially supported by the contributions of its friends and partners.

There were many things in my lifetime that I didn't pursue because I was afraid. I was always great with numbers in high school, for example. I loved accounting classes. Did I get an accounting degree in college? Nope, why not? because I was afraid. Have you done the same thing? How many of us changed our course of study in college because of one or two classes that we heard were hard? We may not have even tried to get that particular degree just because of that very reason.

Recently I experienced a turning point in not letting fear dictate my actions. I was taking an instructor shooting class at a very well-known facility in Arizona. After we had been there for two and a half days, we learned there was going to be a competition. Now, I was one of a class of 25 people. Some of them were army men, police officers, Texas Rangers—men who were way better than I was at this particular shooting contest. But to my surprise I got down to being in the top ten! I couldn't believe it. It was awesome. Then I got down to the top five. Oh, my gosh! No way, then it got down to the top two. Me and a Texas Ranger. Our instructor said, "Take your time and breathe." I was so focused on that target that my heart was beating out of my chest. I steadied myself as best I could. Carefully aimed and took my shot, and I WON! I beat all 25 people! Now, if you had told me seven years ago when I started down this path that I would be in a competition with a Texas Ranger and I would win, I would have said there's no way. I DID THIS AFRAID! And I won.

What have I learned from all of these experiences and many others in my lifetime? Some things may seem out of your grasp, you may think you will "never make it," you may feel this mountain is too high, but my advice to you? DO IT AFRAID! You will never know what you could do if you never try. Why live your life wondering, "What could have happened if I…"? Don't live your life that way. Try at least one thing you are afraid of. You will be surprised at how you feel having accomplished that one thing. It will spur you on to try another thing and another thing and before you know it, your list of "I wish I could" is no more. You've done them all (or some of them)! The point is just do one thing to get yourself started.

THE AUTHOR ALSO EXPLAINS THAT …Fear has no power–it is just a feeling! But it is a strong feeling that too often we give in to. We give it power that it doesn't deserve. It can be a crippling emotion. We need to learn how to overcome it. Yes, some things seem so overwhelming that we will never be able to cope with it (divorce, loss of a child, bankruptcy–the list can go on and on). If you can, overcome it so you can live your life as a freer person, like I did. You could miss some outstanding opportunities by being afraid. I know it can put you in a frozen state–you don't feel like you can move or do anything about it. But you can!

Do you know what the term FEAR stands for? Not what you think! It stands for: Face Everything And Rise!

Concentrate on the good things you have done in your life, not on the things you missed out on. You may need to retrain your brain to find those positive things–I know I did. I don't concentrate on the negative anymore. All the opportunities I will have are because I am not afraid. You will be amazed at what finds you. It's a mindset shift for sure, but it works!

Read Joyce Meyer's book and try for whatever you'd do if you could accomplish it unafraid. It's a feeling that'll last a lifetime. I know I have and will continue to do this very thing. Give it your best shot.

Check out Joyce Meyer's website here: https://joycemeyer.org/

BECKY MOSBRUCKER

Becky Mosbrucker is an advocate for women's safety. She believes safety training for women is essential in today's world. However, she found there were no companies offering services to train women to build the skills necessary to protect themselves. So, she formed her own company: Forward Safety Training, LLC. Training women how to be safe while living a free and active life is her mission. Becky begins with Mindfulness and Awareness classes which she's been teaching for over 20 years. She trains women how to move forward in their journey through life with a positive attitude, while being conscious of their situations and surroundings. She's extremely aware of contemporary concerns for women at home, in the workplace, on the street, online, and in social situations. Becky educates and equips women to be safe in their daily lives. This takes many forms.

She also teaches firearm safety and has many winning titles under her belt. She is always improving her own skills while training others. With her vivacious personality, Becky is also sought after as an event planner on local and state levels and volunteers her time generously with community organizations. She loves the outdoors, working out at the gym, playing with her grandkids, and all things tech!

You can find her at https://forwardsafetytraining.com.

CHAPTER 7

THE LAMP TO MY PATHWAY

by Bridgetti Lim Banda
Executive Live Event Producer, B Live Media
http://www.blivemedia.com

"And you must inculcate them in your sons and speak of them when you sit in your house and when you walk on the road and when you lie down and when you get up" are words my parents took seriously. Little did I know, back then, when I first started reading those words just how much it would shape and impact my life. It protected me from physical and mental harm on more occasions than I care to remember. It also taught me that I needed to forgive up to seventy times seven, but math was never my strong point, so trying to count was pointless. Except it wasn't really about math, even though it taught me never to use scales that cheat because it was a detestable act.

Growing up as a child, apartheid was a system of racial segregation that existed in South Africa. I never fully understood it back then. Coming face to face with people who became tired of being treated like they were second class citizens was a scary experience. People revolted against the government of the day to bring about change in an unprecedented uprising that forced me into situations I could never have imagined. I witnessed acts of violence that would remain with me to this day. It could have been very tempting to join the ranks of those who fought for justice, but the words etched in my mind became my protection as I remembered, "for you are foreign residents and settlers from my standpoint" and "vengeance is **mine**; I will repay." Those words I read, kept me grounded and safe because I knew this war was not mine to fight.

Fast forward a few years. I remember sitting at the edge of my parents' bed telling them I was getting married at the end of that week. My father's words sounded cold and chilling when I was beaming with excitement for my adventures ahead. All he said was, "You make your bed and you must lie on it." Somehow it felt as if my father just threw a bucket of ice over me. Little did I know just how those words would shape and impact the rest of my life.

When I said my vows "for better, for worse, for richer, for poorer, in sickness and in health, to love and to cherish, until death do us part" I knew not to take those vows lightly. The book I read also taught me to deeply respect my partner in accordance with the divine law for as long as we both shall live together on earth.

Marriage is a coming together of two people and families and in my case different cultures. Like many people, I underestimated the challenges marriage would bring. Those early years were tough and the adjustments challenged me in ways I could never have imagined. At times it felt like it may be easier to walk away, but the words of my father kept ringing in my ears. It reminded me that husbands and wives would have "tribulation in the flesh" because we are imperfect. It didn't mean that I became a pushover either. I learned to be balanced because the words, "be wrathful, and yet do not sin" and "let the sun not set with you in a provoked state" guided my thoughts and actions. I learnt that my wows meant that I was not only accountable to my partner but to a higher power. The very one who designed the family arrangement.

To what extent would I trust the one who created me? The one who designed the family arrangement. Never in my wildest dreams could I have imagined coming face to face with making a choice that could mean life or death. I remember lying in my hospital bed the day after undergoing a hysterectomy and feeling so weak, as if someone or something had pulled the plug on me. I was hemorrhaging and losing consciousness. Next thing I know, my doctor was trying to convince my husband to overrule my choice not to have a blood transfusion. Before my surgery, I told my doctor that I had made an informed choice not to take blood under any circumstances. I did not wish to expose myself to blood-borne diseases, possible immune-system reactions, or even human errors. More importantly, because I remembered reading about the importance to "abstain from blood." It was frightening, given that my children were very young, but it was a test of my faith in the one who gave me life. What was intended as a procedure that would require a hospital stay of no longer than a few days turned into a marathon hospital stay. I spent seven days in ICU, three of which I was unconscious, and a total of 22 days in hospital. My adherence to "abstain from blood" ultimately saved my life.

Forrest Gump said it best, "My mom always said life was like a box of chocolates. You never know what you're gonna get." Friendships for the most part come and go. The betrayal of a best friend can hit you like a ton of bricks. When that happens, you really have to dig deep.

What exactly do the words forgive seventy times seven mean? Was it seventy times seven per day, per week, per month, or even per year? As it turns out, it meant that I needed to learn to forgive every time that it hurt. Not to mention trying to count up to seventy times seven each time I felt hurt just seemed impossible. I was obligated to show love and to forgive to the extent of which the one who created me was willing to pardon my errors.

The book I read is God's written Word to humankind. It has shaped my life and I'm blessed to be rewarded with a loving husband, two sons, a daughter-in-law, and a beautiful grandson.

BRIDGETTI LIM BANDA

Bridgetti Lim Banda is a Live Event Producer and Talk Show Host. She helps business owners incorporate live video into their marketing strategy in a manner that results in positive audience-engaging experiences.

Connect with Bridgetti here: http://www.blivemedia.com.

CHAPTER 8

TIMING IS EVERYTHING: HOW TO ACHIEVE MORE BY STARTING EARLY

by Bryan Allen-Smith
Owner, Allen Enterprises
<u>bit.ly/liveawesome2</u>

Most of my life, I've struggled to manage my time. I used to joke with friends that I was so disorganized that I would meet myself coming and going several times a day. Maybe there was too much on my plate, maybe it was not knowing where to begin or how to end, maybe it was lack of planning, or maybe I just didn't take the time to focus on the most important things in life. Regardless, I was a dis-organized mess that was running through life trying to get everything done. I've been fortunate in life to have experienced so many things, but I often wonder if I had been a little more selective, a little more focused, and even a little more disciplined what more could be checked off my bucket list. It's never too late to start and I'm hopeful my story will help you realize what took me almost 45 years to understand.

It wasn't until I read the book *The 5am Club* by Robin Sharma that I began discovering how to organize my time to be more productive. See, life is a series of choices. It's how we organize our time to accomplish the things we set out to do that determines the goals we achieve. To tap into our greatest potential, we must adopt a routine. In the book, Sharma suggests an early morning routine because the first hour after you wake up is your most productive hour of the entire day. For me, that was the key to unlocking the potential of success.

My success didn't happen overnight. In fact, it took several months before I had programmed my body to get up and get going before the sun comes up. It started by setting my alarm for 5am every day of the week – yeah, even on weekends. I would get up, grab a blank piece of paper, divide it into four sections (personal, work, side gig, and development). I'd then take each box and write exactly what I wanted to accomplish for the day. This early morning planning helped me gain insight into everything I needed to do for the day.

For several months, I was disciplined to following this routine. As time went on, I enhanced my approach to incorporate other things that were important to me and would lead me to my goal to #liveawesome2. See, what I didn't realize early on was that it wasn't just about getting up early and creating a list. It was about learning to master a routine that was uninterrupted. I didn't jump up and into technology. This wasn't time to check Facebook, Snapchat, or Tik Tok. It was time to reflect on me and the things I needed to do to get the most out of my life and not allow other distractions to take any energy from me. I know that if you can create this time for yourself, you will accomplish more than you imagine.

Too often, we get caught up in the day-to-day. We find ourselves, or at least I did, reflecting on things that were out of our control. Things that took me back to past events or occurrences that I was hoping to grow from but didn't allow me the space to move forward. One of the principles in the book states that the only way to achieving greatness is to understand that there is only one direction that leads there and that is forward. Taking time each morning before anyone else is awake and before I began any other tasks has allowed me the opportunity to begin achieving things that I am passionate about but also leading me to greatness.

Sharma calls the time from 5am-6am "Victory Hour" because of how much you can accomplish. Now I find myself completing my first hour and having a solid plan that supports the tasks that I want to accomplish during my day. I begin my hour focusing on why. We've all heard that you should think about your why and that is the reason you do things. If your why isn't big enough or if it doesn't lead back to your life's purpose, it might not be worth doing. I know my why and I'm developing a system that works well for me. During my victory hour, I review each task or activity that I write down on my list and I ask myself "why." Why is this important, why am I doing this, why is it going to be worth the time I spend on it, and why will it lead me to my goals. Once I've discovered the why, I can then get into the details of what, who, and how. It seems like a simple concept, but it's worked very well for me.

You may be asking yourself, so why should I read this book? Why should I invest several hours of my time reading the principles that Sharma shares? Why will this make a difference in my life? Well, I can't answer those questions for you. I can share, however, the reason I continue to believe this is the most impactful book I've read recently is because I've seen the results. I understand that spending the first hour of waking to reflect, plan, and apply the concepts of the book, I have seen a big shift in my life. I now respect my time and don't waste it on things that have no meaning or link back to my purpose. The best part, though, is I don't see myself coming and going, rather, I am on a path that leads me to the finish line.

I challenge you to take the time to read the book and think about what you can do to gain your time back. I know for me that I am so much more productive and now have the time and space to live the life I deserve. We all can be more and do more in life.

Good luck and remember, you can #liveawesome2.

BRYAN ALLEN-SMITH

Bryan Allen-Smith has been in direct sales and leadership roles in major corporations for over 25 years. He has been a top producer in several companies and honed his skills while working with Starbucks for over 13 years in a senior leadership role. While he still works in corporate America, his passion for cooking has led him to becoming a Director with the Pampered Chef.

Bryan is currently working on a project to develop and launch a program called "Build a Better YOU" in Fall 2022. The program will help participants tap into their strengths and identify ways to live premium. In his spare time, Bryan loves cooking, learning, spending time with his husband and family, loving on his pets, thriving daily, and living life to the fullest. He wakes up every day with a mission to give more and be better today than he was yesterday. Bryan believes that everyone deserves to live life to the fullest and uses the hashtag #liveawesome2 as the focus for his work.

Connect with Bryan at bit.ly/liveawesome2.

CHAPTER 9

EMBRACE COURAGE AND VULNERABILITY

By Cathy Derksen
Wealth and Success Coach
https://inspiredtenacity.com

"We can choose courage or we can choose comfort,
but we can't have both. Not at the same time,"
Brené Brown

The book that has had a huge impact on me over the last decade has been *Daring Greatly: How the Courage to Be Vulnerable Transforms the Way We Live, Love, Parent, and Lead* by Dr. Brené Brown, researcher and storyteller.

I have read and listened to all of her books over and over again as I absorb her words of wisdom differently each time. The task of picking a favorite book from her collection is a tough one for me. I think it's the combination of her academic approach mixed with her southern sass that gives her such a unique style that I love. Her stories are raw and real and she doesn't hesitate to throw in a cuss word to make a point.

In the past 12 years I have stepped all-in twice to transform my life. I have gone through the challenges of divorce, coping with life as a single mom, two major career changes, and transforming my whole approach to life. Brené Brown's books, TEDTalks, and podcast sessions have been a critical part of my success. She has given me the courage and tenacity to get through these huge challenges in my life and to keep moving forward. She has inspired me to share my story and my journey as a way of supporting others going through similar challenges.

"The willingness to show up changes us. It makes us a little braver each time." Brené Brown

Dr. Brown taught me to dig deep into courage and vulnerability. She took me on the path to deeper self-acceptance and understanding. All of her books are full of stories and life lessons and I keep coming back to them for words of clarity and support as I have made my way through some huge challenges in my life. These times in my life have required me to step into my own story and take hold of courage while being vulnerable. I have rewritten my story and how I approach work, relationships, family, and my own journey. We need to allow ourselves to feel our emotions and acknowledge the pain and struggle we go through. This does not make us weak or less important than others. I have learned that stepping into my authentic self requires being vulnerable and it takes enormous courage.

"Authenticity is a collection of choices that we have to make every day. It's about the choice to show up and be real. The choice to be honest. The choice to let our true selves be seen." Brené Brown

In 2008, my family was involved in a tragic vehicle accident. Luckily for us, we escaped with minor physical injuries. Unfortunately, another man involved was not so lucky and died at the scene. The trauma of this event and the psychological impact was massive for all of us. This was the event that shook my life and gave me the wake-up-call that life is too short and should not be wasted. It gave me the clarity to see how toxic and abusive my marriage had become, and it forced me to see that both of my teenaged children were struggling to find their way in life while living in a toxic family environment. I recognized at that time that it was up to me to take on the huge challenge of creating a better life for all of us.

This series of events set me on the path of personal development and growth. I absorbed the teachings of many amazing thought leaders such as Wayne Dyre, Louise Hayes, Marianne Williamson, Napoleon Hill and, of course, Dr. Brené Brown. Their lessons and words of wisdom have changed my life forever.

With the new skills I developed, I found the strength and tenacity to leave my husband and help my children get back on track with their own lives. In the process of this change, I also found the courage to leave my 25-year career in medical genetics, a job that was very toxic, to set out to follow my calling of helping women create better lives for themselves. At that time, I started a career in financial planning with the goal of helping women take control of their finances. I loved that work, but was held back from really reaching my big goals by the constraints of working in a corporate setting with many rules and limitations on my approach.

In my experience I came to realize that, in order to make changes in our financial progress, we must first allow ourselves to imagine the life we are wanting to create and shift the mindsets that are holding us back from reaching our goals. Working in a corporate setting did not give me the flexibility to address this part of assisting women in changing their life, so I dug deep and found the courage to start the next chapter of my life. I left my job to start my own business that gave me the freedom to help women create wealth and success on their own terms.

Through all of these major life transitions that I have taken on, Brené Brown's teachings have given me the support and clarity I needed to take on my true calling and step into a completely different career with courage and authenticity.

As the founder of my business, Inspired Tenacity, my mission is to create a cycle of wealth and success among women around the world. My programs help women to rediscover their brilliance, and take control of their finances, in order to create the next chapter of their life with inspiration and excitement. In my work, I share the lessons I have learned from Brené Brown with my clients and my community.

CATHY DERKSEN

Cathy Derksen is a wealth and success coach as well as the founder of Inspired Tenacity. Her passion is dedicated to helping women tap into their own brilliance to create lives filled with genuine joy and fulfilment. Cathy's mission is to create a cycle of wealth and success among women around the world. After working as a financial planner for over a decade, she left her corporate job and started Inspired Tenacity to focus on helping women create wealth and success on their own terms. Cathy is also an international speaker and a 5 time best-selling author with stories that inspire the readers to take a leap of faith into reaching for their big goals.

Connect with Cathy at https://inspiredtenacity.com

CHAPTER 10

PERSEVERANCE

by Christina Sorensen

It is often during our darkest moments that we find out how strong and truly blessed we really are. These moments often lead us to courage and inspiration needed to persevere. My inspiration came when I read the book, *The Sun Does Shine* by Bryan Stevens, Anthony Ray Hinton, and Lara Love Hardin. This book altered the way I coped with the obstacles that I was facing in 2019-2020. During that year, I found myself at a low point in life dealing with grief, betrayal, and chronic health conditions.

The beginning of the year began with the loss of several close family members in a short period of time. Initially, I felt numb, unable to think, speak or accept the reality of these unfathomable situations. Furthermore, these losses left me feeling lost, alone, and detached from my daily life. In addition to my grief, I found myself involved in a toxic entanglement where I endured multiple forms of betrayal. This included habitual lying, infidelity, character assassination, meddling family members, verbal, mental, emotional, and financial abuse. Thankfully, this relationship came to an end in 2020.

Another obstacle I was facing during this period was a chronic health condition called sinus bradycardia. This condition caused my heart to beat less than 60 times a minute. As a result, I began to experience extreme exhaustion, dizziness, confusion, shortness of breath and anxiety. In the worst-case scenario, cardiac arrest or sudden death can occur from this condition. In 2020, my heart suddenly stopped for 22 seconds causing me to quickly fall and remain in an unresponsive state for hours. The hospital staff began to prepare a room for me in the Intensive Care Unit but, amazingly, I woke up. Weeks later, a pacemaker was implanted. It is by God's grace and mercy I am here today.

For me, *The Sun Does Shine* began a year-long healing journey. It reinforced the importance of being able to control my own thoughts, emotions, and behaviors in a resilient manner. And the importance of being able to master this ability in a stressful environment that lacked mental stimulation.

It encouraged me to recognize my own unhealthy coping mechanism through self-awareness. I used this awareness to overcome fears, doubt, and self-defeating patterns. I was able to overcome these trials by remaining optimistic during difficult circumstances. In addition, I started to show and practice gratitude for everything in my life through journaling. Furthermore, I began to train my mind to concentrate on solutions with positive outcomes instead of focusing solely on the problems. This book opened the path to seeking out other books, videos, and podcasts relating to my specific struggles. I became better at identifying and verbalizing my emotions and feelings. I was able to set boundaries and recognize my triggers. In addition, I began to take back responsibility for my own self-care.

The more self-aware I became, the more I realized how extremely socially isolated I had become. Some of this was a result of losing many significant people in my life who had been my support system and whom I spoke to on a regular basis. However, with a changed mindset I focused on what I had in the present moment. I was blessed with a large family who provided the emotional support needed during this time. God blessed me with a once-in-a-lifetime best friend. From the moment we met, we just clicked. My children have always been my number one priority, who keep me focused and on track. In addition,

I began to seek support from online groups, and I even sought out a mentor, Sally Larkin Green. Gaining mentors in my life was a truly life changing experience. Sally provided me with personal development skills, became a source of knowledge, emotional support, and helped me achieve goals. I am now able to pass knowledge, information and resources onto other people who find themselves in similar predicaments.

Last, but not least, this book renewed my faith, relationship with God and strengthened my prayer life. Having a near death experience is indescribable, but it changes your focus. I learnt life is too fleeting to be spending it in stagnation. Rather than fretting over hardships, I began to let go and give God all circumstances that were out of my control. All urges to defend, explain or tell my side of the story left me because I know the truth will always prevail. I no longer spend my time reacting or responding to negative situations because life is too short. More importantly, I am learning to forgive myself, forgive others, let go of people and situations that no longer serve me. My time and energy are now redirected towards praying for others that their misfortunes in life turn around. Another valuable lesson I learned is to always give glory to God, never give up, and do not let the hardships redefine you. Instead, use your pain to free yourself and others who find themselves in similar predicaments. I can say that all of these life-changing events occurred after reading this highly recommended book, *The Sun Does Shine*.

CHRISTINA SORENSEN

Christina Sorensen lives in Alberta, Canada, with her two children. At the present moment, she is primarily responsible for providing education for her children at home. This entails creating curriculum, providing instructions, and implementing routines into their daily life. Christina is an avid reader and lifelong learner with a passion in challenging herself to master new skills.

In the past she worked as a legal assistant and private investigator. Christina is also a member of the Metis Nation of Alberta who has advocated on behalf of Metis citizens and affairs. As a mother with a child who has disabilities, she continues to advocate for those who cannot speak up for themselves.

You can find Christina on Facebook and LinkedIn under Christina Sorensen.

CHAPTER 11

PUT DOWN THE BAT

by Dara Bose
Owner, FireWife Boutique, LLC
www.darabose.com

Ivy has been my biggest enemy throughout my life. *Ivy* kept me from doing the things that I wanted to do and from hitting goals I had set for myself. *Ivy* told me things like "you are not good enough," "what makes you think you can do that," and most recently "what makes you qualified to help people, look at your past."

Ivy has a habit of making me feel like I cannot do anything. Yet, I continue to let *Ivy* be part of my life. Most of you reading this would think that I should have let *Ivy* go or tell *Ivy* to mind their own business. And you are right! There is just one problem. I am *Ivy!!!*

Ivy is… ME.

I never really had a name for her before. I often just referred to her as my inner villain. You know it's that little voice in the back of your head that makes you doubt yourself or says unkind things about you, to you. In the book *Self-Bullying: What To Do When The Bully is You!*, the author Sherri Strochecker Leopold referred to that inner villain or inner voice as *Ivy* (Inner Voice–IV-*Ivy*). Since I read her book, that name has just stuck with me. It also makes it easier for me to tell her to be quiet when I start to hear her making those comments.

It can be so easy to believe the negative thoughts as they come. Most of the negative thoughts that we have about ourselves have been engrained in our subconscious mind. We really don't even remember exactly how they got there, but they are so deep into our mind that they seem fact. Unfortunately, some of these negative thoughts are put there by our loved ones when we are children. A parent may tease a child about their weight when they are young saying things like "maybe you should eat a salad" and then the child grows up to have self-image issues.

In my case, I felt that no matter how good I was at something or how well I did it was never good enough. I felt I only received attention when I was a disappointment. It was just how it was for me. I felt unimportant. I was the oldest of six total children between my parents and step-parents.

When I was in high school, I was in the choir and show choir. I participated in the school plays and musicals. I even landed a vocal solo in the last performance of my senior year. It was senior night and all of the seniors and their parents stood up and were recognized at the end of the concert. The choir director called my name and then my parents' names. I stood alone. I had four parents and none of them made it. Of course I was disappointed that my parents did not come, but it was just how things were for me. This moment in time engrained some pretty harsh words into my subconscious programming. I did not even know it at the time. It took me years of personal development to discover this.

I enjoy studying the mind and thoughts. Understanding how your thoughts work and how you can make your thoughts work for you instead of against you is some pretty powerful stuff. I like to examine the conscious and subconscious mind. Your conscious mind being your thinking mind which you can control and your subconscious mind is just on autopilot in the background. I use this knowledge in my NLP Practitioner work as well as my Life Coaching and continue to explore it as I am working towards a degree in Psychology. Our negative thoughts are driven by our subconscious mind. But it really doesn't have to be all that complicated. Sherri explains how *Ivy* works very simply.

She explains the vision of the bat, a baseball bat. We each have a bat at our feet. When we are born that bat is smooth and there is nothing on it. But, as we go through life people begin to stamp words or phrases into our bats. For me, my bat would say "unworthy." When none of my parents showed up for my senior night concert, they told me that I was not worth their time. So, now I have that written on my bat. The more things happen in my life that solidify that thought of being unworthy the deeper the groove gets and the louder *Ivy* becomes.

A couple of years ago I met with a different publisher, signed some papers, and became an author of my own book. During the timeframe of writing my book, the Covid pandemic hit and turned my world upside down. This included putting my book on hold temporarily. But, it was more than just that. I began to let self-doubt and negative self-talk creep in and cause me to start believing that I "wasn't good enough" or "wasn't smart enough" to finish an entire book. And most importantly, "who was I to write a book?" These thoughts that I was having was *Ivy* trying to keep me from my goal of finishing my book. I was struggling. My book was basically done, but I was doubting everything that I had done.

I had a Zoom call with Sherri, the author of the book I read. We were chatting about many things including my upcoming book. I told her that I was still working on it, but she saw right through my excuses. She knew exactly what I was doing. She told me to "put down the bat!" She knew that I was letting *Ivy* speak louder than my purpose. She knew that *Ivy* was telling me that I was "unworthy" and that I was smacking myself in the face with my bat.

Here is the good news! Once you realize you have a bat, you can stop yourself and others from using it against you and she shows you the way.

DARA BOSE

Dara Bose is the owner/operator of FireWife Boutique, a certified NLP Practitioner, Life Coach, best-selling author, and public speaker. She has spent years working on personal development while reaching top rankings in the MLM industry. Through her work in MLM, she discovered her passion for building up other women and her purpose to help them thrive. The wife of a firefighter and mother of three, Dara never ceases to amaze with finding time to support and uplift women in her community.

Whether through participating in small groups at church, organizing fundraising events, and everything in between, Dara represents her best self in all she does. She motivates women to seek their best self through self-reflection, motivation, fashion, and friendship. Women seek out Dara for guidance regularly when working through difficult times, or just needing the support of another woman/mother/wife/business owner. Constantly seeking to better herself and provide the best support she can to others, you can always find her reading a book or attending seminars that build her up and better equip her to share her messaging.

Dara is best known for a saying she uses regularly with her children and friends and can also be applied to anyone in most all situations – "But did you die?" Most importantly, Dara wants all women to know, you are worthy, you are beautiful, and you are meant for more.

You can connect with Dara here: www.darabose.com.

CHAPTER 12

LIBRARIES AND WHAT YOU SHOULD KNOW

By David Blackford
President, Blacklock Designs
www.blacklockdesigns.com

Hello and thank you for being here. I think it's important to recognize and to thank Lynda Sunshine West and her team for allowing the authors within this book the opportunity to share our stories, our favorite books, and what we've learned from them as a way to give back. It was once taught to me that giving of yourself and your knowledge is a great way to keep learning and for that I am grateful.

Before I begin, I'd be remiss if I didn't tell you a little bit about books in general that I have learned over the past few decades and, with that said, my big question for you today is, "Do you have a library?"

Or why would you want or need to have a library?

Well, for starters, your library will become your mental food. Ever hear the saying, "food for thought?" It can be said that books are your food for your brain, just like gasoline is fuel for a car or water is fuel to make plants grow. Now maybe you're not buying that philosophy or my play on words, but I can tell you, it's true. I have seen it, I have lived it, and I have watched others that were succeeding in life and asked, what's your secret? Time and time again I have been told, "Oh, I was reading this book and had this idea." There is nothing more powerful in this world than a good idea.

If you would have asked me 20 years ago how many books I had, I may have said that I had one or two books that someone had given me or that I had picked one up here or there because of the title. But I didn't have a library of books that I wanted to learn from. That all changed in the year 2011, shortly after my father asked me to start a business with him. And as things tend to happen when you start certain laws in motion, a friend of mine shortly afterwards gave me a set of CDs that changed the course of my life.

I'd like to share with you the name of these CDs, because now with the power of the Internet you can listen to them via YouTube. The series is called, *"Your Wish is Your Command."* In this series was the list of books that was recommended reading. I'd like to suggest that you listen to this course to find out on your own and to learn from this master about more than just the list, but if you want the book list you can email me at askdave@blacklockdesigns.com and the book list will be sent your way.

So, what have I learned over the years about books? One, when you go to purchase a book, you should try to find the earliest release date of that book. If you do so, and you're able to buy the book, you will have a book that has within it the original thoughts of the writer. Not revised by someone else or rewritten for one reason or the other. I'd also like to tell you that the use of eBay, thriftbooks.com, and abebooks.com are great resources for finding books at a discount.

Also, don't be stingy on the price of your books because creating your library will be one of the most rewarding things you'll ever do. I remember trying to decide on whether or not to buy a 1937 original copy of *Think and Grow Rich* for $100.00. I hemmed and hawed at the price for more than a day or two, then realized that I had spent way more on college books and I don't even look at or use them anymore. Since then, I realized that this was different, that purchasing these books meant more; that I would be buying these for me, for my library, and that changed the way I felt about it.

Now I know we're supposed to talk about our one favorite, but I want to share that *The Richest Man in Babylon* by George S. Clason and *The Greatest Salesman in the World* by OG Mandino are two of my most read books. Both are stories written in parable form, which I love, and both contain powerful messages and lessons to live by. If you find a good book, it should be read several times. Not in a row, but when you feel compelled to read it again. And why should you re-read a book? If you do, it will reinforce the lessons learned from reading it and something even more magical: when you re-read a book, you will learn new things from it. Not because you missed the significance of the story or a message the previous time, but you will be in a different place and will be open to new lessons for your life. I cannot stress this one enough. If you find a book you like, revisit and read this book over and over again.

A Man from Maine, without a doubt, is my all-time favorite read. It was written by Edward Bok who, at the time of the book's writing, was the editor in chief of the *Saturday Evening Post*. This book was written in 1928 and is the true story of Cyrus H. K. Curtis, who was most famous for establishing and creating the *Ladies Home Journal*. Besides being an example of how to do well in establishing a great company, it provides some of the best tips for business that I have ever read. I love this book and because it was written from the heart, it was carefully laid out from start to finish with care and love. I have purchased many copies of this book as gifts and an autographed original version for my library.

Last note: A mentor once shared with me that behind every successful person that lived in a big old house had a big old library inside of it.

DAVID (DAVE) BLACKFORD

David (Dave) Blackford is the president and founder of Blacklock Designs, an umbrella company and hub for various products. His latest invention: Ancherz® can be viewed at www.ancherz.com. Originally designed for keeping real estate directional signs anchored to the ground Ancherz is currently growing its product line. With a product slogan of, "Because some Objects aren't meant to Move," you know they'll be creating many products in the years to come.

Also, under the Blacklock Designs umbrella, is one special item he sells that is not one of his inventions: A-Leg-Up®. His father designed it to provide a stable and comfortable form to perform tasks such as pedicures, trimming nails, putting on socks and shoes, and spraying foot powder or lotion. If you'd like to view this product, go to www.a-leg-up.com.

If you'd like to view and learn more about David, go to https://about.me/davidblackford

CHAPTER 13

NEVER POO-POO THE WOO-WOO

by Debbie Morton
Founder, Success With Debbie
www.SuccessWithDebbie.com

I used to poo-poo the woo-woo! What did I consider woo-woo? It was the notion that there are energetic forces that we can control with our minds. It was believing in "The Law of Attraction."

Many years ago, someone recommended I read *The Secret*. I bought it, I read it, I thought it was a bunch of hooey. My logical brain simply could NOT accept that our thoughts can create our reality or that we could simply think our way to wealth.

I liked logic not woo-woo. I liked facts, figures, science, and data. For me to believe something is true, I needed to see it, touch it, hear it, or feel it.

Fast forward about 10 years—I'm now an avid believer in manifesting, the law of attraction, and the power of our thoughts to create reality. It wasn't because I read *The Secret* again. It's because of a book called *E² (E-Squared)* by Pam Grout.

I could have read or listened to books until I was blue in the face about the law-of-attraction and how everything is energy. It wouldn't have worked. I wouldn't have believed it enough to even give it a try. After all, you can't see, touch, feel, or hear energy, or can you?

A few years ago, I was struggling in a home-based business I was trying to establish. I would have a little success, but then the success went away. I would try different things, nothing seemed to work. I was spending a lot of money on courses, training, mentors, and masterminds to create success in a business that I would be able to work from anywhere and live a laptop lifestyle.

A mentor of mine asked me to read the book *E-Squared* and it changed my life, and my business. It isn't your typical "how to" or "this is what's so" book. It's more of a lab manual where you are guided through a series of experiments that prove how powerful your thoughts can be.

I'll share just one example; you'll have to read the book to see for yourself why it works, and the other experiments that will prove just how powerful the mind really is.

One of the experiments is to manifest a "gift" that you'll unexpectedly receive. I decided that I would manifest some unexpected money within the next two days. I had no idea how it would arrive, or how much it would be; I just knew when it arrived, I would acknowledge it, and be grateful for it.

It didn't take 48 hours. It took only one day. I found a dime. Now you might be thinking "big deal, you found a dime." I would have thought the same except there were some weird things about this particular dime.

My husband and I enjoy taking walks, and we walk nearly every day. When we exit our front door, we walk across our driveway to the street. We don't ever park in our driveway, we pull both our cars into our garage. We seldom have visitors and no one had come to our door recently. We had been walking across our driveway every day and, believe me, there's never anything exciting about walking across our driveway.

Except…the day after I read the first experiment in *E-Squared* and manifested that money would come to me unexpectedly, a shiny dime appeared in my driveway on our very next walk. It was right smack dab in the middle of our driveway and I have no idea how that dime could have gotten there.

That one experiment got me so excited I read and conducted the remaining experiments and WOW, I became a believer in the power of the mind. By the end of the book, I was sold that woo-woo really works!

After finding the dime that day, I declared that "I'm a money magnet and money comes to me every time I go for a walk." Since that day, my husband and I nearly always find money when we go for a walk. Usually, it's pennies although it was a pleasant surprise that yesterday's find was a quarter.

We don't get rich going for walks; however, finding money every time we do walk is a reminder that what we manifest, happens. If I can manifest small change, I can manifest whatever I want.

Reading the book by Pam Grout proved to me how powerful our mind can be. I thought to myself, why not use my mind on something bigger—my business.

I had struggled for years since closing a brick-and-mortar business to have a successful home-based business. To create a life where I could travel the world and make money from anywhere.

E-Squared showed me that what was holding me back in business was not a lack of skill, lack of experience, or mistakes I was making. What was holding me back was my own thoughts. Each time I set a goal, my mind went into "Yeah-but" mode. Yeah-but it won't work. Yeah-but you don't have the necessary skills. Yeah-but, no one will take you seriously. Yeah-but you're too old, too ordinary, too boring, too (fill in the blank).

I'm still a work in progress and I still want to logically justify the woo-woo. I like to call myself a "practical woo-wooist."

If you are not where you want to be, it's important to understand that you are living your life exactly as you created it. You are a product of your thoughts both conscious and subconscious.

If you don't like where you are, you MUST change your thoughts. You must believe beyond a shadow of a doubt that you can create a life you love. *E-Squared* is a great book that will open your mind to what's possible and allow you to step into your greatness.

If it worked for me, it can work for anyone!

DEBBIE MORTON

After 20 years in corporate America, Debbie Morton decided she would rather work for herself than others. She left her 9 to 5 to buy a failing business that she later sold for 10 times her original investment. She has owned 2 brick and mortar businesses: a metal finishing shop (Powder Coating) and a senior home care franchise.

She's a Diamond leader in the network marketing space where she coaches and mentors thousands of entrepreneurs both on her team (TrifectaELITE) and within the entire company.

She was a top producer in two affiliate marketing companies which led her to be a high ticket closer for numerous "online gurus."

She is an expert in personal development training, online marketing, sales training, and personality training. Instead of DISC, she teaches similar concepts using four birds, which is far more intuitive than letters or colors.

Debbie's passion is helping others succeed. During her entrepreneurial journey she's invested hundreds of thousands of dollars in business ventures, courses, and masterminds. Some worked and were valuable, others didn't and provided valuable lessons.

Whether you're just starting in business, a solopreneur (trading time or products for money), a business owner (leveraging efforts for residual income), or seeking to learn how to preserve and grow wealth through investing, her passion is to help you achieve all the success you are willing to work for.

You can connect with Debbie here: www.SuccessWithDebbie.com.

CHAPTER 14

MORNING ROUTINES ARE ESSENTIAL

by Evan Trad
CEO & Visionary, Team EVAN
www.goteamevan.com

The alarm goes off: *beep, beep, beep...* snooze. Nine minutes later, *beep, beep, beep...* snooze. You slowly open your eyes to see the time. You realize quickly that you have overslept and are going to be late! In a panic, you rush to get dressed, throw together a haphazard lunch, and rush out the door hoping and praying you can get to work on time! The rest of your day is just as rushed. You run from meeting to meeting. You scarf down your lunch. You scramble through each part of your day. Finally getting to bed, later than you wished. Starting the vicious cycle all over again the next day.

This is how I used to run through my days. It gives me anxiety just thinking about it! I never even realized how scrambled my day was. I didn't realize how I was rushing through life and actually not accomplishing anything of substance. I rarely set goals because I just didn't have time for them. I never reflected on anything in my life to think about how it was going because I just wasn't able to. I was always thinking about what was coming next, what I had to do, or what I was running late for. It was like I was just rushing through the motions of my life. I didn't feel successful at anything–my friendships, my career, my love life, and I certainly didn't do anything extra because I didn't have time.

Looking back, I cannot believe that my life was that chaotic. I was busy but could not tell you what I accomplished on a given day. Something needed to change but I had no idea that I needed a change. One night as I was scrolling through Facebook before bed, I saw a friend post about this amazing book that changed his entire day. I was always in admiration of this friend because he was successful and always seemed to have his act together. In this post, he shared how this book transformed his day. Through this transformation, he was able to accomplish more, and still have some free time to himself at the end of the day. I had to learn more so I, of course, went to Amazon and bought a copy.

The book was called *The Miracle Morning* by Hal Elrod. I was so excited for it to arrive and see if I could experience the same type of transformation as my friend. A day or two later when it arrived, I stopped everything and devoured it. I read it in less than a day. As I was reading, I could see how my friend had transformed his day. I was excited to begin my transformation, too.

In the book, Hal Elrod shares a simple strategy that transforms your morning routine to get more accomplished. The routines he shares have you sit in silence, say affirmations, visualize, exercise, read, and journal. As I was reading, I realized how much of a mess my morning was. I learned that your morning sets the tone for the rest of your day. No wonder I felt so stressed out about everything. My morning was a mess!

I took the words and routines to heart and began to slowly transform my day. Little by little, I was changing my morning routine and changing my life. I started with not pushing snooze, but rather when my alarm went off I got out of bed and began my morning routine. I will admit this was challenging for many days, and the urge to push snooze each morning was there. I stuck with it, though. I committed to making the change for 30 days. The more I kept at the morning routine, the easier it got. Soon, I was jumping out of bed and excited to complete my morning routine!

As I kept going, I began to see impacts in other areas of my life. I was becoming more reflective on my personal life and I began goal setting. As I set goals, I began to reflect on my progress daily. I knew the changes I needed to make to continue to reach my goals. It was because of this reflection that I was able to really sit down and make clear changes to my life.

Along with reflection and goal setting, I began to generally slow down. By starting my day with a routine, I no longer was rushing throughout my day. I wasn't always feeling behind. I was, in fact, ahead. I was getting things done at work. I was not late when meeting friends for gatherings. I was accomplishing more than I had ever thought was possible.

I was watching my life transform from chaos to order each and every day that I completed my morning routine. I found myself more happy and also more present with my friends and family when I was with them. I was more intentional in the choices that I was making. I was more thoughtful in everything I was doing. My life was coming together and I was becoming proud of who I was becoming!

To this day, I continue to thank my friend who shared the post about the book on social media because, like him, I also was transformed. It has continued to be a monumental book that I am forever grateful for life because it has created positive effects. I love this book so much that I share it with anyone I know who asks about impactful and meaningful books!

EVAN TRAD

Evan Trad is a distinguished educator and entrepreneur from Chicago, Illinois. Evan's entrepreneur journey began through network marketing where he learned his business management skills. In learning to manage and grow his own business, he realized his passion—empowering people with disabilities.

Evan is passionate about helping people with disabilities succeed in school and in life. He was the founding special educator at a new charter school in Chicago, where, for nearly ten years, he built the special education program from the ground floor and is and continues to thrive today. Evan now works to build a successful inclusion special education program at a high-performing public school in Chicago.

Evan's passion for empowering kids with disabilities and his own entrepreneurial spirit fused together in 2019 when he founded his business Team EVAN. He has the vision that people with disabilities have potential and are more than their disability. Team EVAN passionately develops people with disabilities to be more than and stronger than their limitations, shaping their vision into reality, to become successful entrepreneurs.

This passion spilled over into the world of theater where he serves as president of the board of directors for Tellin' Tales Theatre company, whose mission is to shatter barriers between the disabled and non-disabled worlds, a mission that holds true to Evan's philosophy of empowering others to live the life they deserve.

Connect with Evan here: www.goteamevan.com.

CHAPTER 15

IN BEING VULNERABLE, I FOUND MY STRENGTH

by Farah Ismail
Founder, Interact Consulting
https://www.interactconsulting.in/

It is so easy to keep going on the treadmill of living life the way we think we should live. Our busy-ness gets us going but gets us no-where, it would seem. Why is it so hard to hop off that treadmill and in-stead tread the path we really want to? That little thing called comfort… sounds so sweet, it makes us believe it is all good. It is not, though, is it? Not when it is a zone that contains and curtails our growth.

I was not immune to the comfort zone either. If anything, it kept me stuck in an unhealthy relationship for years. It is no easy feat to end a marriage, even if it is not a healthy one. It takes a great deal of courage. Individuating as a single mother, thereafter, and donning the cloak of a strong woman became my lifeline. In time, these personas became my comfort zone to a fault; I grew apart from my sense of self.

I found the need to be a "perfect mother" and a "perfectly strong woman." The antidote to this perfectionism came years later, when I made a friend at a conference in Tapei. I believe we were destined to meet. She introduced me to a book that became my manna from the heavens. It was *Dare to Lead* by Brené Brown.

"The courage to be vulnerable is not about winning or losing, it's about the courage to show up when you can't predict or control the outcome," she writes. There. This was it. This was what catapulted me out of my comfort zone and into the unfamiliar. Somewhere, the wiser part of me took over, and in that moment of time and space, I decided to embrace vulnerability.

Ending a marriage is often viewed as a loss and my perception was tainted by this view. But in that deep moment where I acquainted myself with vulnerability, I decided that it was a metamorphosis. What had happened in that moment was a rewriting of the story I told myself about a major life event.

Interesting, isn't it, what our minds are capable of? For years, I feared a loss, but a moment's courage had gifted me a metamorphosis. However, no transformation is without its growing pains. Brené Brown's perspective on leadership made me realise I was keeping myself stuck because I was still afraid to be vulnerable.

This revelation might have been a catalyst for my new lease on life, but I had not quite learnt to habitually tap into that courage – courage to be vulnerable. I was, perhaps, trying to prove my worth to myself and so, I had suppressed all the heavy emotions I should have made space for, processed, and healed from. I felt weak and insecure but pretended to be strong and confident.

The year I read *Dare to Lead*, I decided to rewrite my narrative. I would reframe the stories I tell myself. I would listen to the stories I was telling myself and I would build my courage muscles to have those tough conversations with myself. And so, I lived, practised and embodied the lessons I had learnt from Brené Brown. "Where I used to think "I am alone," I would reframe it to *"I am supported."* Where I used to think "I'm not good enough," I would acknowledge that *"I am imperfect and that is human."*

It was not an easy feat, to say the least, but I was determined to give myself every chance to be as authentic to myself as possible. I gave myself permission to experiment, to fail, to unlearn, to relearn.

In breaking the armour of perfection, I found solace. In admitting my weakness, I found strength. In being vulnerable, I found courage.

This transformation brought me to where I am today. I achieved so much more that I thought was possible in my business, family, relationships, health, even community involvement. As a professional who helps organisations and individuals grow, this personal and internal work of mine has become an impetus for my leadership facilitation and coaching.

By the very virtue of my profession, I have seen many other women armoured up, pretending to be strong and confident, when really, they too – as I once was – are losing touch with their authentic selves. A shift in the narrative they weave for their own lives could go a long way in bringing them home to themselves. This became my primary motive in creating my signature 'Unlocking Courageous Leadership Program' and 'Courage to Soar Coaching Journey.' If we can be vulnerable and admit the truth, we can be strong and face every hurdle life may surprise us with. It is my firm belief that if we can own our story, we can rewrite it, too.

"Be brave enough to use your voice, bold enough to listen to your heart, and strong enough to live the life you imagined!"
~ Farah Ismail

FARAH ISMAIL

Farah Ismail is an Internationally recognized Facilitator, Coach, Speaker, and Founder of Interact Consulting. She inspires leaders and entrepreneurs who find themselves frustrated and unfulfilled despite outward signs of success. When they work with her, they re-imagine their business, crafting a lucrative purpose-driven life that delivers more clarity, confidence, connection and meaning.

Having rebuilt her own life and business from scratch after struggling through a couple of life changing experiences, Farah knows exactly how to forge a new path towards a meaningful and abundant life and offers her clients a proven blueprint for success.

In her 25 years' experience, she has worked with global organizations including Johnson & Johnson, Saudi Commission for Health Specialities, Decathlon, Pfizer, Hitachi ABB, British Deputy High Commission, Swiss Re, Ali Baba, Coca Cola, to name a few. Today Farah is passionate about supporting women entrepreneurs and professionals to be brave and purposeful.

You can connect with Farah via email: farah@interactconsulting.in or visit https://www.interactconsulting.in.

CHAPTER 16

"CASTE-ING" MY LIFE; WHAT LURKS BEYOND RACE

by Greer McVay
Owner/Principal, PRECĪS Strategy Group
https://www.greermcvay.com/

I have been told by many of my well-meaning white friends that they do not see color. They want me to know they see beyond the pigment of my skin and recognize my humanity and the personal traits that make me uniquely me. Well, at least this is what I assumed they meant for the better part of my adult life. Like most people, I am a product of my upbringing. I am a mélange of all the influences to which my parents exposed me as I grew up in Berkeley, California, in the 1960s and '70s. I am all that I have been, seen and done, and much of that was a result of the skin I am in. Therefore, I believe that to not see my skin, is to not see me, or at least not all of me. It was during my years of co-habitating with white people (as housemates), that I came to see the world anew: through their experiences. White people simply go through life differently than non-white people, or in my case, Black people, but it was not until I read *Caste*, by Isabel Wilkerson, that I was able to identify, label, and more fully comprehend what it was about my interaction with white people that so perplexed me. Put another way, Wilkerson laid bare my entire co-existence with white people in a way that shed new light on my own interpersonal relationships with people who not only look different from me, but who *are* different.

Caste chronicles the experiences of Africans brought to the "new country," and their journey through the Middle Passage, slavery, Reconstruction, the Jim Crow era, the Civil Rights Movement, and into modern day and "Trump's America." As a child of "hippie" parents— and by hippie, I really just mean "hip" parents, who were "woke" before being woke was a term of art—I grew up with a strong sense of self, a healthy amount of opposition to authority, and a firm belief in my ability to do anything I wanted and was willing to work hard to achieve. I was unencumbered by stereotypes and racialized roles that even in my youth I could see were prevalent in the American south, as civil unrest was broadcast from the deepest, darkest underbelly of our nation, by way of the Edmund Pettis Bridge in Selma, Alabama, and a hotel balcony in Memphis, Tennessee. However, by my pre-teen years, I became aware of a similar, albeit less obvious, but no less prevalent problem percolating in areas like Watts, California, in my own backyard. In fact, my hometown of Berkeley was the epicenter of all things political and thought-provoking, and it was here that I would absorb like a sponge the myriad ideas, art and culture, from which I would form my opinions and frame my world view. It was with this enlightenment that I read *Caste*. I identified with each story, example, and anecdote presented and came away with a new perception of how many of my non-Black friends may view me and perceive my experiences in relation to their own. There always seems to be surprise about my ability to overcome obstacles, big or small, and I get 'atta girls' for accomplishing the minutest of tasks, as if failure is the default expectation.

Wilkerson's *Caste* explains how systems (government programs, etc.) were conceived, established and maintained to benefit, and for the convenience of, white people. From the nation's origins to present day, Africans and African Americans and, indeed, all people of color (POC), belong to what she terms the "subordinate caste" as compared to the "dominate" caste, or people of European descent. Caste is not synonymous with race, class, color or other physically distinguishing traits. Caste refers to the hierarchy, or the prioritization of needs, of people in America, and while a caste system is neither unique to America nor even commonly thought of in relation to this country, it is prevalent in the very systems that govern our daily lives and the way we navigate our world. Studies show policies in housing, banking, policing and even environmental design negatively impact communities of color disproportionately.

We all obey, sometimes tacitly or inadvertently, the predictive roles of our caste and adhere to "norms" in ways that perpetuate the continuation of the very system that subjugates POC. For instance, many withhold ideas in the workplace or refrain from talking out of turn for fear of being labeled the "angry Black woman or man." We inherently understand the historic impropriety of contradicting people from the dominate caste. This minimization of our skills and abilities only reinforces the impression that we are not equal, and it is rarely discouraged or even observed by our professional white counterparts. In fact, it often confirms their suspicions or assumptions about our capabilities. Comments in performance reviews or "family talks" in co-habitating scenarios seem to validate the assessment and justify bias.

Caste is not a book that sets out to provoke hatred or disdain for the "other." Instead, it educates the reader on how we got to where we are. It provides a framework for viewing our current condition and it offers a guide for moving into a better more informed space. As we currently talk about and aspire to diversity, equity and inclusion (DEI) in the workplace and hopefully in our daily lives, we cannot do so without a thorough understanding of the history of race relations in America, and, more importantly, an understanding of how our unconscious and subconscious biases contribute to continued diminution of an entire "caste" of our fellow citizens at the expense of us all. *Caste* draws the reader in through a careful examination of publicly known incidents, laws, codes, and customs, leading to a common base of knowledge from which we can all begin a shared journey toward equality.

It could be said that by reading *Caste*, I was manipulated or persuaded to think of otherwise innocent interactions in a more confrontational light due to the injection, or overlay, of 400 years of racial hostilities into relationships that neither warranted nor deserved the pall that was cast by the unique history of blacks and whites in America. I find it more appropriate to suggest that by *not* reading *Caste*, the opinions I formed would or could have been undermined by the shallowest of consideration of why certain events unfolded as they did. For instance, having my parenting decisions questioned and receiving unsolicited child-rearing advice when the reverse is quickly quashed, might be received as a blatant attempt to usurp my authority and "put me in my place" in a manner that diminishes my child's view of me as a loving, thoughtful caregiver. Viewing such interactions through a caste lens may suggest a simpler, yet misplaced, gesture of assistance, with neither nefarious nor confrontational intent. In other words, it benefits all involved to have a more nuanced understanding of how "un-personal" racially tinged incidents are by understanding how 400 years of assumptions, stereotypes, indoctrination, biases, guilt, desires, and expectations create the conditions where world views merge or clash at particular times in history and skew our perceptions of reality and the roles we play.

In the 2005 Oscar-winning movie *Crash*, several stories about race, class, family and gender are woven together in a masterful exploration of our interconnectedness as our lives overlap. As with the characters in *Crash*, living among white people during the Trump and Coronavirus era helped me better understand how inextricably linked our lives are, and *Caste* helps its reader better understand how the caste into which we are born (dominate or subordinate) exacerbates the challenges we jointly face and how detrimental to our collective success the imbalance is.

We will succeed not because we are the same or because we are different; we will succeed because we embrace our differences as the positive forces they are.

GREER MCVAY

Greer McVay is a dynamic, multi-platform communicator, with a passion for politics, planning and programming. She has proven to be a trusted partner to private clients in her consulting business offering services in Public Relations, Events, Communications, Image and Speaking (PRECĪS Strategy). She also enjoys success as a podcaster, blogger, and is the author of *Sucker Moms*, a light-hearted book on parenting. A sometimes reporter, and a single mother of a college student, Greer gladly accepts most opportunities to share her unique views as a keynote speaker on myriad subjects including family & life balance, the importance of effective communication, and lifestyle, all while weaving in elements of politics, pop culture and her personal passions, which includes travel and all things wine.

Connect with Greer here: https://www.greermcvay.com/.

CHAPTER 17

NEAR AND DEAR

by Jaymie Hale
Reiki Practitioner and Natural Lifestyle Educator
https://facebook.com/jaymiehalengoupa

I felt desperate. Despite praying, hoping, asking, and searching, the insatiable thirst my soul had come to know since my precious mother's passing couldn't be quenched. There must be something more. I started searching Amazon for guidance. Her passing led me on a deeper search for answers to my questions about this life… and what comes after. *Adventures of the Soul: Journeys Through the Physical and Spiritual Dimensions* by James Van Praagh would open doors I didn't know existed. Have you lost a loved one and then felt the subsequent void that lingers without ceasing? It feels as if it just can't be "fixed." The dire longing for answers to the many questions; why them, why in this way, and now where are they? How can I possibly feel their presence again in this lifetime?

Faith was always my foundation; this sad time was no exception. Momma's death strengthened my faith, but I searched for insight and answers. This led to more questions and further searching. Isn't that the way with any great quest? If you've lost someone close, perhaps you can identify with my feelings of desperation for answers and a renewed connection. She was my closest friend in this whole world. The solace I sought was found in the form of a book by someone who has studied death and the souls of the lives of our departed loved ones.

Surprise would have been understating my reaction to this book. Not a traditional source I would have gone to before, but for some reason my increasing need for understanding and my curiosity about this person's perspective struck me. After seeing countless options on Amazon on the topic, I hit the "buy" button and soon opened the door to a whole new set of ideas to ponder.

James Van Praagh has written many books, spanning a few decades, on his personal perspective (and experience he claims to have had) with our departed loved ones. Whether you or even I believe his opinions isn't relevant. Reading *Adventures of the Soul* definitely offered me a different perspective on those who have passed.

My gut told me that if I found answers regarding my Mom, I could also achieve better resolution to the varied life-altering physical health issues that had been plaguing me. They had increased in severity since her passing. There has been much research and documentation on the link between our emotional wellness and our physical health. The extreme grief I had been attempting to cope with for so long had definitely begun to take a toll on my physical well-being. Yet, I felt hope bloom.

In this book, Van Praagh speaks of NOT being a physical body, but rather a soul experiencing a physical existence (life) in the body our souls inhabit. This is similar to many religious and spiritual belief systems. I was not totally unfamiliar with it. The experiences he shares states he believes that our souls have had more than one physical experience, even numerous separate human existences. This is similar to other belief systems that believe reincarnation is the actuality of our souls. James says that we choose to come here because this life is so rich with opportunities to learn, for our soul to grow closer to God, and that this is the underlying purpose of our very human existence.

Have you ever wondered about the purpose of YOUR life specifically? I certainly have. Often. James shares from his experiences of "communicating with the dead," his perspective on this underlying purpose. He believes this life presents circumstances and people which we view as problems or situations that we have to navigate, as a way that produces soul growth. Anything that brings us closer to God causes soul growth. He's not the first person to say this. The *Bible*, as well as many other spiritual doctrines, share such beliefs of "self-improvement" for the betterment of all. Perhaps this is the common denominator in us all. Most of us believe in something. It looks different, therefore feels different, actually feels QUITE uncomfortable in the different-ness. Our beliefs aren't really all that different, as long as we maintain that LOVE is our guiding force. If we are open, seeing and understanding each other's thoughts and beliefs DO differ from one another is not only okay, but beneficial. This book has challenged my way of thinking and what I have known. It presented me with a rainbow striped candy cane in a lifetime of red and white ones. It's not bad–just different. I read this book looking for answers and continued healing and found it.

I've also focused on the purpose of this life, MY life. In reading, a sense of peace was restored. My mind was opened to other ways of thinking about life and death.

Is it bad to have opportunities for growth by being stretched beyond our comfort zone? I asked myself this. Am I required to do as I have always done, think as I have always thought–and do as I have always been told? The simple answer is "NO."

Our journeys, whether joyful or painful, solidify our belief systems. I can choose to be understanding, to comprehend someone's pain and deem their differing views have merit, too.

I have realized more thoroughly from reading this book that everyone's perspective matters and has value, including mine. I feel greater peace now regarding my precious Momma's passing even if it's not in alignment with other people's beliefs. The new ideas learned on the purpose of our time on this earth and the fact we may be revisited by our loved ones' presence is comforting. I have begun to recognize and feel my Mother's presence often. It has taken time and learning to feel connected to her again. Through extensive conversation, prayer, and reading since her passing, I have discerned her presence, and that's due in part to reading this book.

May this bring you enlightenment for the adventures of your soul, too!

JAYMIE HALE

Jaymie Hale is an international best selling author, spiritual seeker, devoted mother, lover of all things natural, reiki practitioner and gentle soul. As a first-time author, she is passionate about providing a read that will encourage and inspire those in need of reassurance. She is a teacher and a light for those who are on a journey through life challenges. As a constant seeker of natural modalities, she inspires others to join her in creating a more natural lifestyle and spiritual growth for a true sense of peace, joy, and love.

Reach out to Jaymie at bookmelove22@gmail.com

CHAPTER 18

BUILT BY BREAKING

by Jennifer Jerald
Founder, Jennifer Jerald Strategies
https://www.jenniferjerald.com

Sitting at my dining room table, staring at the cover of the book just recommended with a promise it would be "life-changing." Feeling numb, stuck, and frozen all while wondering how *this book* would be different. And pondering on all the "why's" that ruled my days.

Why does my life seem so hard? Why do I struggle when *everyone* else is successful? Why is *everything* so hard for me? Why am I *always* fighting with my husband and mother? Why do I struggle with weight loss while it seems like *everyone* else can figure it out? Why do I get so angry when I see something I don't agree with? Why is *everything* directed at me in the worst way?

When will it stop? I can't take it anymore! I am breaking!

A lifetime spent on the woes of my life left me feeling empty, broken, and trapped in a whirlpool of "why's *and* what if's." What if no one likes me? What if I make a mistake? What if they make fun of me? What if I look fat? What if my eye looks wonky? What if I fail?

I took a deep breath, whispered a brief prayer, and began to read. On the inner fold of the cover of this book were listed the four agreements I would learn more about in the next 138 pages. One-by-one each agreement brought an unexpected clarity, just by reading the outline. I was in shock and disbelief, and for a moment, I thought my journey to understanding was complete. Alas, I decided to be more intentional and do the deep dive. I had been sitting in the shallow end of learning for too long. Deep breath… The journey began.

Although the "what if's" and "why's" sneak up from time to time, I can say that this book changed everything. Oh, wait! Now that's a touch unfair to myself. A book is simply a binding with a title and words on the pages. For the book I read to make this kind of a change, I had to be willing to act on the suggestions that came as words on a page.

Step by step the words on the page became ideas for change. I began to practice the agreements individually and felt a shift inside that reflected on the outside in how I interacted with my relationships, both personal and professional. Over time, I shared the agreements with my husband, and we began to add reading them each morning as a couple in our quiet time routine that already included scripture, prayer, and other inspirational reading materials.

The results of this simple practice began to create an even more miraculous shift in our marriage. This shift has created a deeper level of love and respect for each other that has strengthened our relationship. Our disagreements are fewer and farther between and are short-lived, at best, when we remind ourselves of the agreements.

The ripple effect of change has reached our children. Even now, our daughter may catch us in a broken agreement, pointing to the agreements posted on our refrigerator, and with a chuckle we make a quick adjustment to get back on track.

Everything we have ever learned is a form of agreement that we adapt as truth. The greatest gift of this book has been learning that I have the power to break an agreement that isn't working for my good and establish a new one. The hardest part of this transformation was being willing to break in order to build. Was I willing to break old agreements that were stirring the pot of why's and what if's so I could build a better life and start to *live*? The answer was and is an undeniable, "YES"!

Agreement One: "Be Impeccable with Your Word"

The one thing I took from this was to stop speaking ill towards myself. By being impeccable with my word towards myself, the "what if's" about my unique physical traits have diminished and I feel a greater love for myself.

Agreement Two: "Don't Take Anything Personally"

This is HUGE! Instead of becoming defensive because of "how it was said" or even what was said, implementing this agreement has given me the freedom to be myself while allowing others to do the same. I don't have to *change* anything about anyone else. I can focus on me. That's freedom!

Agreement Three: "Don't Make Assumptions"

Oh, my goodness! This ONE agreement changes EVERYTHING! Adopting this agreement has given me the freedom to communicate openly, ask questions and avoid eons of agony, misunderstandings, and suffering. The key to this agreement is to remember to refer to agreement number two when listening to the reciprocated communication! Game changer!

Agreement Four: "Always Do Your Best"

Knowing that my best will differ from day to day based on health, is key. Acknowledging I can do my best, under any circumstances is also so important to the transformation I have had. I don't have to be *perfect*, just simply, my best!

The transformation of myself and my family from the incredible message in this book and the steps we have taken to implement is the difference between:

- Surviving in fear and **Living** in **faith**
- Surviving the next fight and **Living** in **love**
- Surviving the next breakdown and **Living** with resolve **to build** up
- Surviving the why's and what if's of yesterday, today, or tomorrow and **Living** in **today**

There is hope for change when we are willing to take steps in the direction of change. Thank you, Don Miguel Ruiz, for writing your amazing book, *The Four Agreements – A Practical Guide to Personal Freedom*. Our lives will never be the same and that is a good thing! Thank you for creating a practical way to be built by teaching us to break first! Your world of change is one book, one page, one word, and one step of action away! Read "The Book I Read" today!

JENNIFER JERALD

Jennifer Jerald is the FOUNDER & CEO OF JENNIFER JERALD STRATEGIES. As a woman who has embraced and learned to live with Borderline Personality Disorder, Jennifer now empowers and transforms women who feel they have no control in life, have no confidence, and are emotionally overwhelmed by identifying by identifying and implementing simple steps to create and maintain emotional freedom, otherwise known as boundaries. She has also gone on to author 5 Bestselling books centered around emotional wellness and healing.

Jennifer shares her love of music and passion for performing by using original songs during her motivational speaking events, podcast interviews, and TV appearances. Her voice carries clarity of hope and triumph through powerful spoken and musical stories.

A fun fact about Jennifer is that she has two different colored eyes. Be sure to follow her green eye. The brown one is always looking for other opportunities to serve.

Jennifer is affectionately known as The Boundary Hunter™.

You can connect with Jennifer at https://www.jenniferjerald.com.

CHAPTER 19

HARRIET, MY HERO

by Julie Brown
Leader, doTERRA
https://www.facebook.com/julbro

I shrank under the covers and shoved the flashlight under my pillow when I heard footsteps in the hallway. Mom would not be pleased that I was still awake on a school night. I froze in the darkness and feigned sleep as she cracked open my bedroom door and checked on me and my sleeping sister in the other bed. I then listened for her bedroom door to quietly close and I eagerly grabbed my flashlight and lit the pages of a book that was so riveting, I couldn't bear to put it down. At the age of 12, my world was opened up to a story so fascinating and stirring that it would change for the rest of my life my view of humanity, following your dreams, and how to be a better person.

Mr. Perkins, my sixth grade teacher, had offered extra credit for reading a book from a historical book list. I found myself drawn to *Harriet Tubman: Conductor on the Underground Railroad* by Ann Petry because she was a woman and most of the choices were about men. I was eager to learn about a woman who had an impact on history. And she was black. That also intrigued my young mind.

I lived in an all-white neighborhood with a few Hispanic families nearby and the only African American I'd ever met was Curtis, a camp counselor I made friends with on a three-day trip to San Francisco when I was ten. He was so kind to me, I assumed everyone of his color was much like him. Getting to know Harriet through her harrowing story only further helped form my elevated opinion of black Americans. As a child, I knew nothing of racism.

As I turned the pages, I was shocked to learn of man's inhumanity to man. I could not understand cruelty, slavery, or people being persecuted because of the color of their skin. It did not make sense to me. It shook my belief of fairness and goodness in the world. But more than that, I found a hero, an inspirational woman who was courageous, selfless, and born to be a leader. Harriet Tubman became a role model to me and her biography changed my life in the sixth grade.

A tenacious little girl, who was made to slave all day in a cotton field, had a dream. She was determined to rise above her circumstances. I remember how I had been sad my parents couldn't afford to send me to dance lessons to help me realize my dream of becoming a dancer. The best my mom could do was call me in to watch Bobby and Sissy dance when The Lawrence Welk Show was on tv. I did my best to follow along, flinging my arms and legs the best I could to imitate their moves.

But a little girl from the 1800s influenced me to believe I was in charge of my own dreams. Born and raised on a southern plantation, Harriet had a dream to run away and find a life of freedom. Her tenacity and vision inspired me to boldly start a babysitting service so I could pay for my own dance lessons. It was stressful when the beginning of the month neared and I didn't have enough to pay. But I was determined to make it happen and I did.

Although Harriet risked everything, even her life to live out her dream, her example of strength and courage has inspired others for hundreds of years to believe in themselves and take action to create their heart's desire. She taught me to work, to dream, and act on what I wanted. Eventually, I became a professional dancer and later ran my own dance studio for 20 years. None of this could have happened if I had not dared to dream what once seemed out of my reach.

Choosing a role model like Harriet Tubman would mean I could never measure up to the scope of her accomplishments. The "Moses" of her people, she braved every danger and overcame every obstacle to free souls from the horrors of slavery. She is one of the bravest and most admired women in American history. Her own liberty was not enough. She daringly worked tirelessly to save others. She is one in a million and deserves the hero's crown.

I wondered how could I be brave? How could I make a difference? I determined to stand up to the bullies of the world in my own little corner of the sky. With determination, I became champion of the underdog! That meant sitting by the boy at lunch who smelled bad. It meant there were no boundaries in my circle of friends. It meant standing between the abused and their bullies. There were social and physical consequences to my small acts of courage. But it was nothing compared to the heroism of Harriet Tubman.

Her selfless quest was dedicated to helping others. She risked her life and her own freedom to save her people. Caring not for her own safety, she braved perilous journeys leading others out of bondage. Freedom was too precious a gift not to share. She was fierce in her mission and relentless in her conviction to make it happen…a more selfless woman, I have never known.

What did I learn about being selfless? Thinking of others and serving their needs was all I could think to do. Kindness and service was always on my mind, but not easily delivered in any measurable way for a girl who didn't have much to give. All I know was a woman who never learned to read or write became one of the noblest people in history. From her, I learned to make dreams happen, be brave, and think of others first.

My path as a youth was filled with mistakes, but I do believe I was better having known Harriet Tubman, my hero, from the book I read.

JULIE BROWN

Julie Brown, author, speaker, and recruiter at hubTEN Global, is passionate about making the world a better place by collaborating on many projects to bring people together to share their gifts. The world is a better place when good people inspire and create together.

The grateful mom of five terrific grown children, the happy wife of the handsome Kirk Brown, and grandma to the five cutest kids on earth, home is where Julie hangs her heart! When she isn't orchestrating family fun, she may be practicing the piano or volunteering at the local food bank. She feels called to head up personal history projects to help her loved ones become unforgettable. She has helped publish three histories and is currently working on two more. In years past, she was a professional dancer, choreographer, and studio owner. She is now content to attend productions as an enthusiastic audience member. Julie's entrepreneurial spirit is satisfied in her leadership in doTERRA and sharing natural solutions to heal the mind and body. Helping others create wealth and healing has brought her much joy. Julie and her family reside in the beautiful state of Utah where they relish having four seasons.

Connect with Julie here: https://www.facebook.com/julbro

CHAPTER 20

SO THAT'S WHAT IT WAS, I WAS NOT A COMPLETE FAILURE!

by Julie Donelson
Founder & Creator, Julie Donelson Brands, LLC
www.juliedonelson.com

I have been a voracious reader my entire life. Since I consider myself an introvert, and can be quite shy around people I don't know well, reading is the perfect hobby! But it wasn't until a few years ago that I read a few books that profoundly changed my life for the better.

As a child, student, college student, even as an employee, there were areas of my life I could not seem to manage, no matter what I did. I became overwhelmed with clutter, particularly paper clutter. I always wrote notes to myself about everything–books to read, movies to watch, things to see, do, visit, my mind racing, and what felt like a million swirling thoughts all... the... time.

I never thought anything of it. I tried to be more organized. Tried ALL the planners. Still, I'd have notes (thank the gods for the sticky ones!) all over the place, tucked into my planner, on the table, even to this day I use them on my kitchen cabinets for specific things. But, rather than go down a path of decluttering–that's a subject that requires MORE time and space–let me tell you how this book, in conjunction with a couple others, have transformed how I feel and how I function on a daily basis, and how I learned that...

1. I was not a total failure at life.
2. To lean into my natural tendencies and traits and made them a superpower.

Now let me be honest, I still have paper. But not like before! I was practically buried in it. At one point, I was in an office at my job, it was perhaps 6 feet by 8 feet, quite small. There were paper piles on the desk, under the desk, covering the bookshelf, filling a file cabinet, and even stacked in "organized" piles on the floor to the point this little office looked like it was FULL! I mean, I still have a vision of it in my head and it makes me shudder. It was so depressing to go to that every day! It weighed me down. It felt like physical weight I had to carry around. It stifled my thoughts and ability to get my work done.

It wasn't only that mess. There were other things, too. A large amount of debt. Excess weight. A messy home with just TOO MUCH STUFF that I couldn't get a handle on. Laundry piles that got washed and dried but rarely put away. A home that I could never keep picked up. We aren't talking just a messy dining table or mail counter. I'm not a hoarder by any means, but it was all just leaving me feeling every single day like I was failing at everything. Plus a hundred projects all 'in process,' and equipment from a dozen or more hobbies I wanted to do, but never seemed to get to.

And all the time. More ideas. More things to start. More things to buy, or make notes about.

I Was Exhausted

Until I happened upon a time in my life when I was involved with an organization that encouraged its members to read personal development books. And then take what they learned and use it to make their life better. Well, who could say NO to that?! Not me. I've always loved learning anyway. I was the kid who enjoyed school. Even if I didn't seem organized, I was intelligent and capable. Since that time, I've read dozens (maybe hundreds) of personal development books, attended workshops, seminars, branched out into other areas like business development, and so on. I still have hundreds of ideas, and many notes, but here's what has happened over time. I learned that all the things I was thinking were simply quirks of being 'me,' were really symptoms of ADHD.

The book I read was called *Women With Attention Deficit Disorder* by Sari Solden. This book was a revelation for me. It gave me so much information, it reassured me I was not a failure, that it was my wiring that needed support and that I was not broken and seriously flawed. This book, combined with a few others I will name for you, ALL worked together for me to have so many insights, revelations about myself, and gave me concrete ways to CHANGE the things I could that it made a huge impact on my life, my relationship with my husband, and literally changed my life for the better. I now have a deeper understanding about how my brain works, how to leverage my thought process, how to recognize what's working and not working, and how to move my days forward with intention, preparation, and ease, so that I am not overwhelmed to the point of inaction and living in a perpetual state of mess.

I am happier, more confident, have less guilt and shame about myself, and can respond to life events in more productive ways. I've been able to USE those oddities to my advantage. I've paid off debt, started my business, minimized our home (or closer to minimizing) so that the amount of items I have to manage are reduced, in turn, making chores MUCH faster and simpler to finish. I've had the added benefit of feeling better about our home, because it is clean and less messy. Anyone who stops by unexpectedly now doesn't leave me completely embarrassed because of the condition of the living areas. Now my crazy dogs are another story–they have a lot of love for visitors! Whether visitors want it or not!

Some other books that have added to my transformation are:

The Four Tendencies by Gretchen Rubin
Atomic Habits by James Clear
Tiny Habits by BJ Fogg
The Miracle Morning by Hal Elrod

I could go on with a few more, and if you like, you can find me on Instagram and Facebook where I often share about books.

JULIE DONELSON

Julie Donelson is an MSW and certified Transformational Coach. She coaches women to help them get what they want and say YES to the life of their dreams. Her self-guided mini coaching course will be available spring of 2022.

Connect with Julie on her favorite social sites, Facebook and Instagram or her website at www.juliedonelson.com.

CHAPTER 21

YOUR ANSWER IS ENERGY

by Dr. Kim Jacobs Martin
Founder Clinic Director, North Shore Health Solutions Ltd
www.NorthShoreHealthSolutions.com

The Answer Is Energy: A Thirty-Day Guide to Creating Your Ideal
Life, Embracing True Abundance, and Knowing Your Worth From
Within by Jarrad Hewett provides thirty chapters of personal stories,
guidance and daily meditation that reveal how to shift energy and reframe our inner thinking. Some topics are about our interpretation
of money, relationships, fear, control, passion & purpose, abundance,
to live in the moment of now. I am always looking for a great teacher
whether it is in the form of an audio, book or a class. I find myself
drawn to these topics because I feel I am always trying to improve. I
first read this book cover to cover. I like a lot of what he had to say. I
highlighted paragraphs that I wanted to come back to at another time.
What I learned from reading this book is that these lessons take time.
The second time I read this book, I made notes and took my time to
understand why each topic was strong and powerful enough to be one
daily activity. Sometimes I could "hear" what each lesson was trying to
teach me and I was able to make an energy shift.

That simply means that I am able to resonant with Jarrad Hewett
who is a spiritual energy expert. He has a way of explaining how to
quickly shift into a paradigm of love, ease and abundance.

When someone's energy is in alignment with their true intention of being healthier, happier, and more productive, great empowerment and life-changing transformation occurs. As we get older and have different experiences, this book helps a reader to clear up, forgive, and not let their inner negative programming affect their current situation.

I think about the time when I go home after a long day at work. I would light my favorite Nag Champa incense, grab a Pellegrino and relax on the couch with my four fur babies. I can look around my home and smile and feel happy. I love the quaintness of my home. All my stained glass and Asian art mixed in with the "Painter of light" oil paintings of Thomas Kinkaid. I have come a long way. All by choice. I had negative patterns that no longer served me. When I read the daily chapter and write out what my take-away is from each day, and read the meditations out loud, I am purposely aligning with a positive energy shift.

A few years ago, I would come home and skip enjoying my Pellegrino or incense and prefer to just go upstairs and watch tv. I was not in a happy place. I felt the energy was sucked out of me after working with patients all day. I was helping people every day! When was I going to help myself? My way of re-charging was ignoring everyone. It wasn't until I got back into journaling and reading what I wrote that I knew I wanted to make changes and it had to start with me.

I have become selfish with who I choose to allow into my energy field. If I go to a party and the energy is negative, I have no problem leaving. If I have a patient who is not willing to take some responsibility in their health journey and blaming others or blaming their other doctors for the side effects of their medications, I have to release them from my practice. I have the choice of who I want to help.

How many times have we read something or heard a great piece of advice and we can't wait to share with anyone who will listen? That is how I feel this book has helped me. I am getting ready to read this for the fourth time for the next thirty days and I already know that I will be making energy shifts. That doesn't mean that I will be changing thirty days in a row. It means that depending on what I am experiencing daily can make me think differently. This book is not a one and done philosophy.

Chapter 11 is all about change. Change is scary. Change is the unknown. Change can be good, but we have to be willing to let go of the negative thoughts. It doesn't mean it has to be hard. It's our thoughts about everything being hard, so we just don't try. We want that scary thought to be an "exciting adventure."

According to chapter 21 "The Brain," we have the power to shape that energy through creating new dimensional pictures through our thoughts, actions, and most importantly, our feelings. Feelings are the gasoline in the engine of manifestation. This means that when we know how to change how we feel we can make long-lasting changes.

I also knew when I started reacting differently to things I used to look at as a negative feeling, that I had made that energy shift and I was able to forgive, move on in a positive manner. I had to make a conscious choice how I was going to react. I felt empowered. That's when I knew I learned how to make the energy shift.

Your mindset is powerful. It can change how everything in you and around you looks and feels. It teaches you to be preventive instead of being reactionary. That is what I tell my patients. We want your health in a prevention mode instead of reacting to diagnostic tests that confirm a condition that we could have prevented.

I know this will be a book that I will be reading again once or twice a year.

If you do the daily lessons, you can use this book as a roadmap to help understand who you are and what changes you want to make. We are all made up of energy.

In summary, this book has taught me to be the captain of my own ship, and to know that we are never too old to make changes.

DR. KIM JACOBS MARTIN

D r. Kim Jacobs Martin, DC has over 24 years of experience improving the lives of her patients, using an all-natural holistic approach. She takes time to analyze your symptoms and develops an overall wellness plan, getting to the root cause of your health concerns. Telemedicine is available.

Connect with Dr. Martin, DC here
www.NorthShoreHealthSolutions.com.

CHAPTER 22

WHEN YOUR SOUL SPEAKS

by Kim Kelley Thompson
Founder of Kim Kelley Productions and
The Successful Startup Summits
www.KimKelleyThompson.com

Sadness is a funny thing, it can hit you at once or slowly creep into your psyche like mold growing inside a wall. I tried to run from pain, thinking that if I could get far enough away, to an area of wide open space with plenty of room to breathe, I'd somehow be healed. My mom once told me that her parents took her to the Cape when she had pneumonia, trusting that the salty air would heal her. That memory stuck with me as I packed my car and headed towards the mountains praying to breathe my own healing air.

I had always trusted my instinct. Chronic ear infections as a child taught me to listen to my inner voice. But now, I began looking outside myself for answers, for hope and a sign that life as I knew it would return to 'normal.' Just what was 'normal,' I was no longer sure.

Somewhere between my parents' divorce and my brother's addiction, my soul had hardened. My faith crumbled and my trust in God and myself vanished.

I questioned everything and everyone. "Were they telling the truth?" "Just what do they want?" "Why should I trust you?" I was beginning to approach every encounter with a hidden fear.

My days were filled with the joy of skiing. My evenings were filled with work and a busyness that kept my thoughts at bay. I knew both were an attempt to escape the questions and anger that occupied my mind.

I lost myself. I was certain of that. I cut off the friendships that were once important to me. I shut down my feelings, they were too painful to acknowledge. My solace had always been found in nature and this time was no different. It was nature that comforted me, here I could breathe easily, silencing the anxiety and panic attacks that tried desperately to grab my attention. The beauty of nature signified that there had to be a power greater than man at work behind the scenes. Almost like a director calling out cues from backstage. But what were those cues? "What am I supposed to do now?" "How do I move forward and let go of this pain?" I must have asked those questions a thousand times.

One day my dad came to visit, we spent hours skiing and talking about the future – my future. We rarely spent time discussing the past, there was no need, it was gone. Feelings? What feelings? I learned that life isn't always easy or fair, just pick yourself up, move on, put one foot in front of the other, and so I did. My dad was in sales, and it seemed rather easy and fair. He spent 90% of his time on the golf course, yet somehow he was quite successful. "Well, if that is possible," I told him, "then my future must be in sales, sign me up!"

During one of his visits, he gave me a book by Og Mandino, *The Greatest Salesman in the World*. That book quickly became a favorite, I read it several times. It slowly began to reinstate my faith in God and my belief in my own self. I always knew He hadn't left me, but I just couldn't understand how He could let bad things happen.

That one book started me on a journey of personal development. I began reading and listening to every self-help book I could get my hands on. Books like *The Power of Your Subconscious Mind* by Joseph Murphy, and *Your Erroneous Zones* by Dr. Wayne Dyer.

But there was one book, a small essay actually, that opened my eyes to the inherent wealth within and my responsibility to understand it. The book: *Acres of Diamonds*.

A seemingly simple book, with the moral that wealth and opportunity are all around us. Yet, that book carried a much deeper meaning for me. It taught me that each one of us is right in the middle of our own *Acres of Diamonds*. Our answers are always within. I had been trying to run from my feelings for so long that I completely shut down my ability to trust. I no longer knew myself. I lost the dreams I once held and along with them my belief in God.

This book helped me see that I did have my own acres of diamonds. It enabled me to realize that no matter how determined I was to ignore my feelings, no matter how busy I stayed, or how far I traveled, my mind would always be with me. It was the same mind that once trusted its own intuition, the same mind that had faith in a greater power, the same mind that once cultivated an incredibly vivid imagination. This mind, my mind, was my acres of diamonds. I had a choice. I could choose to grow where I was planted, face my feelings, and allow myself to actually feel them, or I could continue to run and live with doubt, anxiety, and panic.

I'd like to think I had this incredible aha moment, that I'm a fast learner, but it took me a bit of time to realize that the breakup of my family led me on a path of self-reflection and discovery. It also caused an unraveling of the religious dogma I had grown up with and replaced it with a spiritual appreciation. I began to see that the solution to everything I was experiencing, the answers to all those questions I'd asked over and over again, my true peace was inside me. It didn't matter if my parents reconciled or not. It didn't matter if my brother chose sobriety. I could not control things outside myself. I tried, oh did I try. But I could finally see and accept that pain can be a fantastic teacher, if we are willing to look for the lesson. I learned to recognize, thank, and cultivate the diamonds within my own soul.

KIM KELLEY THOMPSON

Kim Kelley Thompson is a business and personal development coach who provides entrepreneurs with the strategies and support they need to turn their business dreams into reality.

She stresses practical application, not theory, teaching new and struggling entrepreneurs the same tools and techniques that enabled her to build a thriving production company and online publication attracting advertisers such as Marriott and Hilton Hotels.

Having raised four children by herself, while managing a multimillion-dollar event company and starting her own business, Kim is known for simplifying the process of business building.

She takes an inside out approach to her teaching, focusing on both the mental and practical steps that build momentum in business. She is a firm believer that personal development and business development go hand-in-hand.

Kim believes that we all have unique talents and abilities along with desires which we absolutely can achieve once we know the steps to take. Desire drives action and action creates clarity. Her work helps people clarify their ideas and create the action steps to achieve them.

Kim is blessed to be a mom, entrepreneur, speaker, author and founder and host of The Successful Startup virtual summits, and the soon to be released Successful Startup podcast.

Connect with Kim here: www.KimKelleyThompson.com.

CHAPTER 23

HOW A MATH TEXTBOOK SAVED MY LIFE

by Kohila Sivas

"Everything is solvable when you get hooked by the introduction."
by Kohila Sivas

Creator of the Revolutionary MathCodes Method
https://www.mathcodes.com/

On the afternoon I said goodbye to my dear grandparents, I didn't know why they cried. But they knew something I did not—that it would be our very last embrace. I was six years old.

That day, my family fled the civil war in Sri Lanka and emigrated to Canada. My dad was determined to get us to safety, and he did. But he had lost everything. And that broke him. Soon after we arrived, he began drinking. The violence started. I always felt unsafe at home.

My life was in turmoil. Everything was a struggle: language, culture, racism, and there seemed to be no relief. School was hard because I barely spoke a word of English. And I resisted learning. So, I was very quiet and very alone. I hardly spoke a word in class. Then another relative broke my trust. For me, every day of my life was complicated and seemingly out of my control. There were things I simply did not understand.

By the time I was thirteen, I was exhausted from the pressure—both at home and at school—and wanted nothing more than to stop the pain. I tried to escape, but I was resuscitated at the hospital.

School was painful, and I struggled. Especially with math. I became an expert at looking busy and I'd do anything to avoid the teacher. I'd copy the textbook into my notebook and look thoughtful. I'd study the posters hanging on the walls. I read one quote by Albert Einstein hundreds of times before I considered its meaning,

---

"It's not that I'm so smart. It's just that I stay with problems longer."
~Albert Einstein

Finally, those words stirred something deep down inside me. I thought of how easily I gave up on problems. I began to think that if I let math beat me, I would not become the person I could be.

I'd always been a systematic thinker. I constantly searched for the "why" behind everything. So, instead of resigning myself to becoming a victim of circumstance, I started asking if others could do it, why couldn't I?

I committed to spend more time with math.

That day when I opened my math textbook instead of going directly to the assigned questions, I began to read the introduction.

And there it was—the magic.

That introduction captivated my imagination thoroughly.

For the first time, I learned the history of how a rule was discovered, how a concept was developed, and how it connected to the real world. It was exhilarating. Right away I read the next chapter, and then the next and the next.

I learned about mathematicians who never gave up and about their motivations. I felt like I was right there with them as they struggled to discover concepts and advance our world. I learned WHY math was created, why it was developed, and why it is important.

Those introductions inspired me.

For the first time ever, I felt motivated by the challenge of math. I finally saw the *value* in learning formulas, concepts, and rules. I even daydreamed about Pythagoras and Einstein sitting with me and describing to me how they figured them out.

And so it began. I would sit with a single problem for hours. I wouldn't give up.

I discovered math in context to my own life. I always looked to see where and how it could be applied. I searched for math in every experience, and in everything around me.

And I developed my own stories to help memorize and recall concepts and rules. Soon I began to find success in class. My math teacher noticed and offered to help. For the very first time, I stepped out of my shell. I even began to ask a few questions.

The thrill of achievement was intoxicating. It was new for me.

But most importantly, math was comforting. I couldn't control my own life, but math was predictable. When I worked through a problem, I was in control from the beginning to outcome. I found solace in the logic and order of the system. It became my escape.

Soon, math became like a game. I felt like I was "hacking the secret codes" of a puzzle. That was when I really started to excel. My process of reverse engineering and solving seemed so simple, and I began to wonder WHY teachers made math so complicated.

It was THAT question which inspired me to become a teacher and, later, a private math coach.

Math saved my life, and it changed my path, but it all started with one textbook introduction. Math gave me the confidence I was missing, and a stability I never knew. Math broke me out of my shell and transformed my life. Math was the reason for new friendships, and it provided me with a sense of purpose, and ultimately financial freedom.

I graduated high school with an A but, more importantly, a profound love for math, and a mission to become a different kind of teacher.

I knew what was important was to develop inspired, lifelong learners, not just students working for grades. I was motivated to inspire students to see math as something exciting to learn. I wanted to teach them how to use failure as a guide for success. I wanted to teach them how to take control and escape the victim loop, to be committed and accountable, and to develop good habits. I wanted to teach them HOW to learn. Because learning math will change any student's life for the better.

And that's exactly what I do now.

KOHILA SIVAS

Over the past 23 years, Kohila Sivas has worked in the classroom at every grade level. More importantly, Kohila has worked privately one-on-one with over 1,500 struggling math students because there's a huge difference between classroom curriculum delivery and transforming an unmotivated struggling student who 'hates' math into a student who loves math. And that's her mission today.

Kohila has distilled the teaching of math into a series of shortcuts, hacks, and easy to memorize and recall stories which are transformational. These she refers to as 'codes.'

Her company, MathCodes, trains other teachers and tutors. She continues to work with struggling students. And it's all thanks to Einstein and to the many math textbooks that Kohila still reads to this day. Kohila is hooked on math forever.

Connect with Kohila at https://www.mathcodes.com.

CHAPTER 24

THE BOOK THAT SAVED MY LIFE

by Kristy Boyd Johnson
Joyful Creator at Living Creativity
https://www.starseedjourneyretreats.com

"The words that enlighten the soul are more precious than jewels."
~Mazrat Inayat Khan

What book has changed my life? This is a tough one because I'm an avid reader with a deep and abiding love for wonderful stories, well-told.

I have read so many books that had a deep and lasting impact on me. As a child, my favorite book was *A Wrinkle in Time* by Madeline L'Engle. I traveled by tesseract with Meg and Charles Wallace across space and time to battle the shadow of IT (something that is strangely pertinent in today's wacky world). Another all-time favorite is *Illusions* by Richard Bach. That story appeals to everything in me that knows we are so much more than we appear to be.

But for our purposes, my choice of life-changing book is *The Artist's Way: A Spiritual Path to Higher Creativity* by Julia Cameron. This book is designed as a workbook to take the reader on a journey of self-discovery. Cameron's wonderfully authentic voice created a sense of safety while I transitioned through three significant periods in my life.

The first time I worked through *The Artist's Way*, the process saved my life. Literally. I was trapped in an abusive marriage to a manipulative and conniving narcissist. A dear friend gave me this book as a gift because she knew I dreamed of being a writer but was struggling with the toxic gaslighting my ex heaped on me. I got to the passage about "Crazymakers" and it was like the author shined a big, bright, Truth spotlight on my heart.

That was my life, and I did not like what I saw.

"How have I allowed him such control over me?" I questioned myself. "I've let a crazymaker make a mess of my life." Instead of backing away, or burying my head in the sand, which is so tempting to do, I faced it. I kept working my way through the book, writing my morning pages every day (which incidentally I hid under the driver's seat of my car – a place he would never look). I didn't know it, but I was healing even though I was still enmeshed in that life. I began to grow, and little by little, I emotionally separated myself from him.

And everything got… So. Much. Worse.

I understand now that he could feel his control slipping. All abusers and bullies, from individuals to huge corporations and governments, do the same thing – they try to crush you with more control and more manipulation BECAUSE they know they are losing you. And he was no different. I barely slept because I had a strong, intuitive sense that he was planning to kill me. He terrorized me daily, and I knew he was working up to carrying out his threats.

The final showdown came one day when, in the face of one of his vitriolic attacks, I called him out on his lies. This time, something in me just… shifted. He came after me, expecting me to go lock myself in the bathroom like I always had before when the fists started flying. Instead of hiding, the Viking warrior woman in me emerged, sword drawn and hair on fire. He threatened to get his gun, but in that moment, I didn't care. I snapped.

"Go ahead, coward!" I screamed, "I dare you!"

I saw the fear deepen the lines in his ugly face. He turned and ran. I chased him out the door. He didn't return until the next day, and by then, it was all over but the signing of the divorce papers. He could not get away from me fast enough, which was just fine by me.

The second time I worked through *The Artist's Way*, I ghostwrote my first book. Cameron's wisdom helped me transition through all the fears and doubts that had been instilled in my mind by my not-relevant-anymore ex-husband. My client loved my work, told others, and I was able to supplement my dismal teacher's salary with some amazing ghost projects.

The third time I worked through *The Artist's Way*, I wrote my first children's book. I had been taking Improv classes and having a lot of fun. One summer night, a June bug flew into our room. Anyway, some of the ladies were all, "Eek, a bug!" Not one person moved.

So, I shushed the June bug toward the door. One thing about me – I talk to myself. Aloud. (Just part of being an auditory learner, an introvert, a cat lover… and a big nerd.)

I said to that little green June bug, "Let's go outside. You'll be so much happier out there with your friends." The June bug flew toward the door, stopped in the doorway, and hovered there, looking at me.

"Oh, come on," I said. "You know you want to."

And out it went.

I closed the door to prevent further encroachment by June bug, only to find my Improv group staring at me, open-mouthed.

"She's a bug whisperer," came an awed whisper. They started applauding, so I took a bow.

As I continued my *Artist's Way* journey, my first children's book idea dropped into my head, fully formed. It's the story of a boy who can talk to bugs, which is a fun premise for all kinds of shenanigans. I'm re-releasing this book in the summer of 2022, under its new title, *Doofus*, along with the first book in my *Lily Star, Monster Hunter* series.

My well-worn copy of Julia Cameron's megabook *The Artist's Way* still sits on my bookshelf today. Sometimes I browse through it for inspiration or encouragement, but when I'm ready to dig into a project, I'll open my veins and bleed through the process again. Every time I do, something big happens in my life, and it's ***always*** a change for the better.

KRISTY BOYD JOHNSON

Kristy Boyd Johnson can't imagine a better life than one spent in beautiful locations with wonderful people who are making life joyful for everyone.

Connect with Kristy at https://www.starseedjourneyretreats.com

CHAPTER 25

FORGIVING: EVEN WHEN IT SEEMS 'UNFORGIVABLE'

by Krysten Maracle
Retired
https://www.facebook.com/krysten.maracle

Never Give Up!!

My goal for the amazing readers of this chapter is to relay that it is never too late to have a happy, fulfilled life. Even when it feels like all the cards have been stacked against you at any given time during your life. To assist you in finding happiness and fulfillment, I will also share a few strategies that have helped me.

As an incest survivor, from the age of 3 to 13, it took me a very long time to feel worthy and loveable. My biological father abused me, verbally, physically, and sexually on a regular basis and my mother never protected me. I believed deeply that if my own parents didn't value me, no one else could value me. I wanted to feel honored and cherished by my parents, but I would settle for anyone.

Luckily, I "escaped" my abusive father when my parents divorced and my mom's new marriage moved me across the United States from California to Pennsylvania. However, I found out very quickly that distance does not heal the bitterness and sadness within. I tried to prove myself through accomplishments in both academics and sports, attempting to heal the void. During all four years of high school, I played varsity tennis, varsity basketball, and ran varsity track while being a member of the National Honor Society. Unfortunately, even these accomplishments did not even begin quench my low self-esteem. Why???? Maybe it was because I was still hiding the "family secret." Maybe it was because my father never called. Not even to say Happy Birthday or Merry Christmas. Nothing! All I wanted as a child, growing up, was to matter! I wanted to feel worth something! I wanted to be loved by my father. Instead, I felt separated from him without closure, validation, or love.

I was a pioneer woman in Computer Science, in 1987, obtaining my bachelor's degree from San Diego State University. I was a member of Upsilon Pi Epsilon (UPE) Honor Society, participated in 20+ years of therapy, read many self-help books, raised two children, Kaitlyn and Nathan. They both graduated Cal Poly, San Luis Obispo, and I retired after 30+ years from the Navy Information Warfare Center (NWIC) located in San Diego in the Cyber Security Department. And still, I felt the need to be validated. I needed to know I was enough!

It wasn't until recently, in 2021 at the age of 57, when I read *Ho'oponopono: The Hawaiian Forgiveness Ritual as the Key to Your Life's Fulfillment* by Ulrich E. Duprée, that I finally got the "memo" from GOD!

In this book, it discusses "aloha" and the 4 Magical Sentences:

I am sorry.
Please forgive me.
I Love you.
Thank you.

Aloha means "I see the divine in you, and I see the divine in myself." The above 4 short sentences are both a meditation and a prayer. The book discusses that judging people who have done wrong only hurts the "judger." One must be in harmony with others, and not feel separated.

Today, I feel closure through forgiveness by practicing the aforementioned 4 Magical Sentences.

In addition, I learned to give thanks for *EVERYTHING* that has happened in my life. The good and the not so good. I write in my gratitude journal in the morning and evening to remind me of all the good that happens each and every day. It doesn't even need to be a big event. It could simply be, "I am grateful for a hot cup of coffee on this cold, rainy day." Most importantly, I "train" my mind to shift from resentment to *freedom of forgiveness* by repeating these 4 Magical Sentences 10 times, each day, in the mirror.

Since reading this book, I know that I am worthy, just for being born. I repeat the 4 sentences to myself when my inner critic is being less than positive.

Please try this exercise for yourself, if or when you are feeling low. To stop the negative thoughts immediately, just pause... and say these 4 Magical Sentences: I am sorry; Please forgive me; I Love you; Thank you.

Yes, it is that SIMPLE!

I have learned that everyone, including the mentally ill, pedophiles, murderers, etc. need grace and forgiveness. Only through forgiveness does healing prevail. No amount of accomplishment will fill the void caused by holding on to pain.

Another strategy is to remember that feelings are just that! FEELINGS! I am now able to question and discern my feelings and emotions. When possible, I encourage you to take the time to analyze your thoughts and determine if they are fact or emotion based on old stories. Many times I have found that my inner critic plays old tapes which are no longer true.

Today, it is extremely important that we realize that WE MATTER as suicide is very prevalent in our society. Astonishingly, 22 veterans, every day, take their lives. This number doesn't account for the non-veteran deaths by suicide either. When I was 35 years old, I lost my only sibling Bryce, who was only 37, to suicide.

My mind started swirling with guilt and thoughts such as, "I should have talked to him more," "I was not there for him," "What more could I have done?," "Why did he not call me?," "Why did we never talk about the sexual abuse?," "Why did we never prosecute our father?," "Why? Why? WHY?"

The *simple* answer: Money and time. How much would it cost and how long would it take to convict? Not to mention, my brother and I never even discussed what had happened to us. The *real* answer: I avoided it, for fear that rehashing the past would consume more of our lives because of our father's sinister acts.

Unfortunately, I will always wonder if I had had an honest conversation with Bryce if I could have saved his life. Survivor's guilt was in full-swing and again I have had to learn how to forgive–myself and my father.

If you are not feeling well, emotionally, and find yourself going down a deep, dark hole–question your thoughts regularly and often. You will learn that your mind is not always truthful and usually thinks the same way as it did in the past. However, you are NOT your past. I challenge you to not let the PAST define you. Once you recognize this, you can and will deliberately improve your thoughts. Your mood will follow, and you will feel better.

Always remember, it is not what one has been through, but more importantly forgiving those who have mistreated or harmed you. Please do not allow the past to define you. You are much greater and stronger than you realize. You were born to be YOU! Please keep your joy and inner peace and do not allow anyone to steal it from you. Continue to look for angels in your life. They are everywhere.

I hope and pray that by sharing my experiences with you, it has given you hope and inspiration to live a more purposeful and happy life through forgiveness. "Better late than never."

Please join me in my Facebook group "Maracle 'LIVE' Mastermind" which is intended to give HOPE to others in honor of my late brother Bryce. Please feel free to contact me thru Facebook messenger if you would like to connect or have any questions.

Stay Safe, Stay Healthy, and Stay Blessed.

Namaste!

KRYSTEN MARACLE

Krysten Maracle was born in Point Loma of San Diego, California, and graduated from San Diego State University with a Computer Science degree with Honors in 1987.

She worked as a navy civilian at Navy Information Warfare Center Pacific in Point Loma for over 30 years, retiring from the Cyber Security Department in 2019.

Due to Krysten's upbringing as an Incest "thriver," she has a passion to help women achieve their goals regardless of their traumatic past and wants all women to know that they are WORTHY just for being born.

Because Krysten has lost so many close people to suicide (her only sibling, brother Bryce, her maid of honor, and other close friends), Krysten wants to share HOPE to all people, young and old. Everyone matters and deserves to thrive and find happiness. Krysten has discovered that forgiveness is key.

There is always a new day, EVERY DAY. Never give up!

Today, Krysten is a speaker and Best-Selling Author of the following books:

Power of Proximity; Wealth Made Easy; Momentum: 13 Lessons from Action Takers Who Changed the World; and Invisible No More; Invincible Forever More!

Connect with Krysten here: https://www.facebook.com/krysten.maracle.

CHAPTER 26

WHAT THE BLEEP CHANGED MY LIFE – A JOURNEY INTO THE UNKNOWN

by Latara Dragoo
CEO, Ideal Marketing Solutions Inc.
https://idealmarketingsolutionsinc.com/

I remember when I saw the movie *The Secret*. It changed the way I saw the world and opened my eyes to the Law of Attraction.

This seemed like just a small piece to the puzzle. But it set me on a path of self-examination and improvement that I have been on ever since.

My exploration of similar knowledge led me to a book called *What the Bleep Do We Know!?™: Discovering the Endless Possibilities for Altering Your Everyday Reality* by William Arntz. That was another huge gamechanger. I feel like saying this book changed my life is an understatement. It literally changes the way you perceive the world around you–like you are seeing it with fresh eyes.

Interestingly, the book was written after the movie of the same name. However, the book is a lot more in-depth, and dives "down the rabbit hole" as it were. (I would recommend getting the audio book, as it involves a lot of dense scientific research and description...or simply watch the movie to get a broader overview of the book's contents.)

This is filled with the kind of knowledge that you can't unlearn once you've heard it. Understanding that the concepts behind the ideas of the Law of Attraction and Vibration, mind over matter, etc. are actually based on the scientific discoveries of quantum physics and integrating these findings into our whole reality creates a new paradigm, and a new way to view the world. We are not just cogs in a machine; we are co-creators in a fluid and organic universe. We can influence things not only on an atomic level, but on our very experiences in life.

The Secret is a great introduction into this kind of new approach to viewing and interacting with reality. *What the Bleep Do We Know* sites example after example of how the principles laid out in *The Secret* have a scientific basis.

It also illustrates how things like Spirituality, Religion, Science, Philosophy and Chemistry all were founded from the same fundamental needs of man–wanting to know and understand ourselves, nature, and how we can harmonize with it. Due to historic events, there was a split between spirituality and science, but it doesn't have to be that way. They are both two sides of the same coin, and the coin represents our aspirations to make the unknown the known. As we learn more about Quantum Physics, we realize amazing correlations between ancient religious views and the way the universe really works.

So how did this change my life? Many ways. This resets the parameters of the paradigm in which we live. Understanding that there is a very real, scientific basis for the idea that we create our reality, gives way to exploring that in a real world application. I have been working on my own ability to create my own reality. While I am a novice, I am still an eager student.

I used to be very down on myself. I would have horrible internal dialogues—putting down my actions, my behaviors, and [lack of] intelligence. One of the most memorable revelations from *What the Bleep Do We Know* was about Dr. Emoto's water experiments, in which containers of water were labeled with different words, such as "Love" and "Evil."

Drops of these waters were frozen and the resulting structures were viewed under a microscope and documented.

While words like Love formed beautiful crystalline structures, words like Evil formed disturbing blobs.

After realizing the damaging effects of negative self-talk, and, conversely, how positive vibrations can have a physical impact, I have been much more conscientious about my internal dialogue, and have also paid attention to creating a positive environment. These things include having written affirmations posted in visual places around the house, listening to high-vibration music, removing toxic relationships from my life, and more.

While I do still run into instances where I am kicking myself for mistakes I made, I am getting better, and devote myself to constant improvement in this aspect.

I was so inspired by Dr. Emoto's research that I created "Manifestation Mugs." These are cups with uplifting words on them such as "Happiness," "Love," "Peace," and "Gratitude." I am currently selling them online on my site, LOA Outlet.

Another aspect of an entire life-changing event that stemmed from reading this book was based on the idea that we are hardwired to cling to the known, rather than dive into the unknown, even if we are miserable in our current situation, and even if there is a very strong possibility of stepping into a much better situation.

Taking this knowledge very seriously, I have taken my life in a very drastically huge change in direction and have faced the unknown full on. I left behind an 18-year long career and started my own business. I basically let go of everything that was "known" to me and took a leap of faith. I am moving to another state, 1700 miles away, and am now in an entirely new set of circumstances.

As of the time of the writing of this chapter, I am sitting in my friend's living room, working from my laptop, looking to buy a lakefront dream home.

Did I make the right choice by leaving behind everything known, to embrace the unknown, create my own reality, and choose my own fate? Only time will tell. But I did it! I conjured up the courage to go for it. I would love to connect with you and you can follow me on my journey, and see if my bravery pays off.

LATARA DRAGOO

CEO of Ideal Marketing Solutions Inc - Helping you Brand Like a Billion-Dollar Company! Graphic Design & Marketing Strategist, Latara Dragoo helps small business owners and coaches increase their online presence and attract their ideal clients.

Latara has over 18 years of graphic design, branding, and marketing experience and has worked with companies such as Eric Lofholm International, Dream Homes, Berkshire Hathaway, Pacific Sotheby's, Haute Living, Marilyn Hoffman International, Discover Magazine, and more.

You can reach Latara here: https://linktr.ee/Latara.Dragoo

CHAPTER 27

A CONVERSATION BETWEEN FRIENDS

by Legend Thurman
DVM Candidate
https://amazon.com/author/legendthurman

Similar to a large portion of children and adolescents in society, my upbringing consisted of going to church every Sunday, saying grace before meals, prayers before bedtime, and the typical proceedings one can imagine for a Christian family. More specifically, I was raised Roman Catholic and received a Catholic education through middle school and again when I went to college and attended the Catholic University of America in Washington, DC. What rooted in the beginning in simply living a good, Christian life transformed into a formal awareness of moral ethics, spirituality, the foundation of the Sacraments, and theological development throughout history.

My involvement in religious activities increased over the years, too, and by the time I graduated college, my resume consisted of serving as an Altar Server, Lector, Eucharistic Minister of Holy Communion, teaching Children's Liturgy, and working as a receptionist and associate in several different departments for the largest Roman Catholic Church in North America. You could say that I was established in my faith and well-rounded in its immersion in my life as I also took proper time out to attend mass daily and add on a theology minor to my undergraduate degree. However, being a child of God and having a well-rounded understanding did and does not negate the fact that I am human and constantly am curious to comprehend ideologies further. One of the most frequent and valid questions you will hear atheists or agnostics ponder and even those who believe in God ask is: "How can there be so much evil in the world and bad things happening on a frequent basis if there is such an all-powerful, all-loving God?" I will not lie that this question has crossed my mind at points in my life as well, that is, until I read *The Shack* by William P. Young in 2019.

Anyone who has ever come across this powerful novel will be familiar with its origin of a man who is married with a beautiful family, possesses hidden scars from personal, familial trauma in his past, and the suffering he endures when his youngest child is abducted and murdered while away on a camping trip. Mackenzie, the main character, during what is referred to as "The Great Sadness" in the story, spends a weekend at the shack (the place where his daughter died) meeting God in the form of the Holy Trinity (Father, Son, and Holy Spirit). While I am not here to give you a book review as to specifically what happened at different points during Mackenzie's encounter with God, but more so to share how the conversations impacted myself on a personal level.

Depending on who you ask, the definition of "good and evil" usually varies based on life experience, upbringing, or personal virtues. I have found that as a society we label something or someone as "evil" based on destruction, abuse, violence, and tragedy, be it personal, professional, economic, or politically related. However, something that the Holy Spirit recalls in this novel is that good and evil are constantly in competition with one another and that we as humans are inclined to have a great capacity to take on the responsibility of declaring what is good and what is evil.....Isn't that a solid truth, though? When there is an absence of light, life, and love, we define it as "evil." On the other hand, God is pure light and love, and when He is removed from our lives, it is then that we tend to be lost in the darkness, incapacitated and restricted by bonds holding us back from seeing the bigger picture. During the first book

I was involved with as an author (*Invisible No More; Invincible Forever More*), I shared my story of progressing from invisibility to invincibility, but despite growing during this time period, there were numerous occasions when I found myself simply asking: "Why?" and questioning not only God's purpose in my life but for the rest of humanity, too. *The Shack* was one of the first pieces of literature next to the Bible that outlined not a road of hardships and turmoil, but a renewal stemming from the mystery of life itself. We, as humans, make choices every day that impact our own as well as others' circumstances. Therefore, if the possibility of consequences were absent, then there would be no room for love to blossom. For God's motivation is to weave a greater good out of our lives which includes our sorrows. Our choices are not above His divine and all-powerful purpose.

The other facet sits in a great big room called "judgment." Because humanity fails to process the mystery of God in his own essence during times of turbulence, it is for this reason that we tend to ascend to our own thrown and act as the judge, insisting that we play the role of God. I am sure you all are in my boat when I ask if you felt that God was punishing you in some manner for a choice that you made or an event that occurred at some point in your life and are still facing personal repercussions because of it. I cannot count the number of times I have stared up at the ceiling at night debating that idea. Nevertheless, *The Shack* reminded me that God's heart is not longing for us to suffer but rather take the work of evil and transform it into love for the greater good. We expect a pain-free world, but no one is immune from evil as long as it has a way in through free-will, a gift from God that traces all the way back to the deception of Adam. Instead, we need to focus on trust in lieu of trying to wrestle with the idea that we are damaged goods.

The external and internal parts that we carry so well can still be heavy, so do not be afraid to reach out your hand to be carried home.

Be at the center of love and purpose. As an individual who has always felt closest to God when she is serving on His altar combined with past feelings of unworthiness at different stages in her life, the perceptions of this book have aided me in providing a framework to my relationship with God...to which there are no rules, only a deep and meaningful trust that is never forced but enlightened. We were never meant to complete this journey alone; instead, all it was ever meant to be was a simple conversation between friends.

LEGEND THURMAN

International #1 Best-Selling Author and a native of Washington, Pennsylvania, and Washington, DC, Legend Thurman is currently a Doctor of Veterinary Medicine Candidate at the Royal Veterinary College aspiring to be a governmental veterinarian advocating to give a voice to those who cannot speak for themselves while being rooted in servant leadership. Featured with the AVMA, SAVMA, DVM360, Vets for Success, Vet Candy, Women Action Takers, and more, some of her previous work has included animal/veterinary legislative initiatives, public policy, and advocacy on a local, national, and international level.

Legend is also a firm believer in overcoming some of the struggles humanity faces in terms of acceptance, self-image, vulnerability, and imposter syndrome among veterinary professionals and society as a whole. When not working on her degree, you can find her at the Basilica of the National Shrine of the Immaculate Conception in DC, traveling, or spending quality time with those she loves. She is set to qualify in July 2023 and plans to move back to the USA to carry out her mission of creating everlasting change for all creatures great and small in alignment with the AVMA Agenda.

Connect with Legend here: http://linkedin.com/in/legend-thurman

CHAPTER 28

MY SOUL'S JOURNEY

by Lorrel Elian
Intuitive Mentor at Lorrel Elian
https://www.lorrelelian.com/

"I would rather live in a world where my life is surrounded by mystery than live in a world so small that my mind could comprehend it."
~Harry Emerson Fosdick

Have you ever wondered why you're here?

I have. So many times. I never imagined I'd find the answer.

I would be remiss to not acknowledge my biological family for ostracizing me, kicking me out of the clan, when I thought I needed them most. This actually has been the greatest gift I could have ever received. It gave me the motivation I needed to heal my body, my life, and discover my Soul's purpose.

I filled my heart, my mind, and entertained my lonely evenings as a single mom. Books became my entertainment, then my lifeline. Through them, I discovered new ways of looking at the world. I came to understand why my life looked the way it did and found peace with the family I was born into. I believe we have two families: our biological family and our Soul family.

Books have always been my guides and travel companions. Many to this day are worn out just from traveling with me. Being pulled out of carry-on pouches, sliding across car and plane seats, landing open faced, upside down. Bindings broken and curled up corners from heat, humidity, dry and cold climates.

I now understand why the books in Bali all came in plastic sleeves. A beautiful paperback of Kali, the goddess of destruction, started turning green from mold before I realized why she needed her plastic protection.

I knew I had special talents, long since buried by life. I couldn't see then that I would rediscover them through precious manuscripts. My life was so mundane and lonely. I spent way too many hours wondering why I was so unloveable.

Each level of discovery came through in chapters of coded mystical messages linking me to other times, other lives.

Have you ever wondered if Earth is the only plane of existence?

Visions and memories started coming forward, as I educated myself through the mystical lives of others, who dared to write about other worlds and their experiences.

I was called a rebellious teenager. For sure I acted every bit of it. 'Crazy' was referenced a time or two. My parents did their best, trying to get help for their out-of-control child who ran away and had all manner of adventures.

Looking back, I was actually running forward, searching for not anything I could put into words. I knew in every fiber of my being that I was not where I was supposed to be.

Jokes amongst siblings about my potential adoption had me wondering. I didn't think they would bother to adopt such a nuisance of a child.

I found courage, and intuition, through the guidance and stories of authors, whose books helped me to find my way. I outwardly may have looked crazy, but on the inside I was a soul searching for my tribe.

So many of my inspirers felt they didn't belong to their blood family. Conflicted, even tortured, by their attempts to fit in.

Lack of acceptance to the tribe makes us do crazy things.

What happens if you don't fit in?

Some of the most memorable stories are of heroes being forced from the tribe. Even Buddha left his wealth, community, and family to discover who he was. In *Autobiography of a Yogi*, Swami Yogananda's life helped me put aside any doubts I had of mysticism and magic. I felt I wasn't alone in my crazy imaginings.

Today, as an Intuitive Mentor, I use my own heroine's journey to inspire others to let go of the past, discover their purpose, and live more consciously in their body.

One of my spiritual teachers scolded us for being lazy to fix ourselves, and for expecting society to do it for us.

I played that card for a while. There's no glory in being the victim. Healing your life, being the best version of yourself, whatever your circumstance, is a choice. "Put your feet to action and do the work," I heard often. There isn't a pill.

The more I worked on myself, the more life changed. My body got stronger, health conditions improved. The healthier I got, the more my intuitive gifts came through.

I still don't refer to myself as psychic. I believe we're all born this way. We are connected through source energy. That's how we know.

My first granddaughter just arrived and all the messages she sent ahead over the years are filtering in. I see magic every day.

All the nuances of her personality are revealing themselves to me from her birth numbers.

I received so many messages over the years, and now that she's here, proves to me that magic is real. The universe is where life comes from. It's all a big math experiment. The numbers will guide you if you learn how to work with them.

Studying Feng shui with a teacher from China is where I first saw how, the moment you are born, links you to your environment, using your birthdate as a guide for life.

I studied different systems till I found Dan Millman's *The Life You Were Born to Live.*

Our purpose is to live fully and consciously in this vehicle called a body. Dan's number system has helped me to understand human dynamics and body energetics.

If you don't know what your purpose is, pay attention to the messages your body is sending you.

Your body plays a role in helping you to understand your purpose and what you're here to do.

All the experiences you've had are teaching you how to be the best version of yourself.

If you've had trauma, learn from it. Don't stay in it.

The more painful your life is, the more important it is for you to take action. Pain is a great motivator, and often that's what it takes to inspire the transformation we're here to experience.

Today, I know I'm exactly where I'm supposed to be. Each moment, purpose filled and intentional.

"Om Mani Padme Hum"

Buddhist mantra meaning "The jewel is in the lotus."

At first I didn't appreciate the sanskrit name chosen for me by my beloved teacher. Kamala, means lotus in full bloom. A symbol of rebirth and enlightenment, the lotus rises up out of the mud every morning to return to muddy waters every night. I see now how wisely she chose for me. I am Kamala.

LORREL ELIAN

Lorrel Elian has a deep understanding of Body Mind Communication and how that works in relationships: personal and business.

She's an internationally accredited teacher of psychosomatic therapy, Master face reader, Therapist, yoga teacher and creator of Somatic Face Therapy.

Lorrel's been an entrepreneur for 30 years. The past decade has been dedicated to the science and application of human connection, through physiology, epigenetics, and genealogy. She is passionate about living healthy and considers herself a 'Self Care Activist.'

Lorrel incorporates a spiritual approach in helping women who struggle with confidence and feeling authentic in their business, to discover their purpose through what they do. Lorrel's known as the Client Attraction Queen for her unique communication training in body language messaging to help entrepreneurs find their ideal clients.

She believes Relationship building is an art form and your business is Art.

Her side passions are:
-The ocean & paddle boarding

- Practicing Hatha yoga
- Yamuna Body Rolling
- Xcountry Skiing
- Salsa, hiphop & ballroom

She lives in the heart of Canada with her husband of 25 years, Larry, and their furbabies. Larry and Lorrel are plant-based foodies, organic landowners, and grow their own food.

Some favorite sayings:

"How you do one thing, is how you do all things."

"Body first, then business."

Connect with Lorrel here https://www.lorrelelian.com/

CHAPTER 29

PERFECTLY IMPERFECT, NO APOLOGIES NECESSARY

By Lynnette LaRoche
Founder, Lynnette LaRoche LLC
https://thelarochemethod.com

The school playground was my refuge from being told "no," "you can't," "you're not like this," "the bible says you must," "you must shun the ways of the world." It was the time I could play and run wild with abandon. To be free. Me.

My most favorite thing to do in the playground was to swing. I would swing so high that I could see above the school building. Then I would bail out in the air and land perfectly on both feet. In these moments, my classmates admired me. It was a time when I was one of "them."

I loved anything that required agility and fast movement … be it skating, biking, Chinese jump rope, dancing, or running. I loved these activities because it felt like it could free me from my constraints. But, everything … stopped.

As I moved into adulthood, the unfamiliar world around me was like a vise. In order to breathe or find release, I felt that I had to force myself to contort to fit the environment in which I was in at the time. I lost myself. For decades.

For more than three decades, I chased fitting in, looking for where I belonged, looking to be accepted. So, I pretended to be who I needed to be to fit in. I said "yes" when I wanted to say "no," just to belong or be accepted. I would smile on cue and say what they expected to hear.

My new world was equally as hard as the old world in which I grew up. I was existing, but not fully living. I had been hiding myself from the world, but also from myself.

I had always been into learning, to keep improving my skillset. But in my mid-fifties, I started my self-development journey.

When I picked up the book, *Girl, Stop Apologizing* by Rachel Hollis, dang, right in the introduction, she called me out by saying "women are afraid of themselves … if we weren't afraid of ourselves we wouldn't spend so much time apologizing constantly for who we are." And "we've got to stop living in fear of being judged for who we are."

I bought the book in 2020 when a member of a Facebook group had mentioned it in a post. However, I wasn't yet ready to read it. I did not read it until January 2022! The title alone was impetus for me to read it as it spoke directly to me. I read. I highlighted takeaways that I have printed to refer to from time-to-time.

Key takeaways for me, especially as an entrepreneur, included stop worrying about what others will think about what I am doing/pursuing; stop invalidating my worth by saying what I am pursuing has already been done before, so I should step back; stop "subconsciously" deciding that I will fail before even trying; stop seeking permission for pursuing my dream; and importantly, stop allowing people to talk me out of my goals, my dreams. These were more colorful threads in my self-development tapestry.

Since I had grown up with so many rules (the Bible), the first thing I did was stop putting rules on my life because they were inhibiting freedom of expression of self and inhibiting my life.

I started saying "no" when in the past I would say "yes" to retain "acceptance," even when I did not want to do that very thing. I started saying "yes" to myself. Over and over and over again.

I started taking responsibility for myself and what I desired to create in my life and stopped worrying about being judged. Rachel had said that many times we assume people are saying the worst things about us, so we let that assumed opinion govern our lives, but it is really in our own thoughts because most times we have no evidence of these dissenting opinions of others.

I stopped primping to be liked or accepted.

I stopped apologizing for what I want, why I do what I do, and for who I am, and to embrace who I am, unapologetically.

Whilst going through a home renovation at the time of this writing, the experience brought to mind something that Rachel said in the chapter on Effectiveness. I was hee-hawing on not having an environment conducive to growing my business, that the disorganization had caused too much dysfunction for me to operate. Rachel had said that if we need perfect conditions to be our best, then we are not in control. We have to create the environment that allows us to be in a space of creativity no matter where we are.

A few years ago, I ceased my pursuit of perfection. It was debilitating. But it was Brene Brown's definition of perfectionism that really brought it home for me. She says in *The Gifts of Imperfection* that "Perfectionism is a self-destructive and addictive belief system that fuels this primary thought: If I look perfect, live perfectly, and do everything perfectly, I can avoid or minimize the painful feelings of shame, judgment, and blame."

Brene goes on to share that when we seek perfectionism, we are more likely to experience emotions that lead us to blaming ourselves when we or things do not go as planned. This was definitely me. I was constantly blaming myself for everything that did not go well, never seeing the many more things that had gone right, only seeing where I could have been/done better.

No, it is not my fault. I did nothing wrong. I do not have to apologize. I needed to be compassionate toward myself. I've made peace with the process that my home is going through as it is a reflection of me and how I am continuing to transform in my journey. I am going all in on my dream.

I am still working through not being afraid of myself, my power, but I have full awareness of the greatness within me and the impact that is before me to make in this world.

LYNNETTE LAROCHE

Lynnette LaRoche is a holistic transition strategist and high-performance coach, building upon 25 years in the biopharma/biotech industry where she was known for building high performing teams that successfully achieved corporate milestones.

Thus, it was a natural progression for Lynnette to start her own business, focused solely on helping the underserved women over 50 to step into their entrepreneurial rising through her signature The LaRoche Method program that empowers women who are either ready to break free of the golden handcuffs or ready to retire from corporate, to rise up and create businesses that fuel their passions so that they can live the life of their dreams.

As a high-performance coach, she helps women overcome burnout by helping them achieve whole-life integration, as well as help women master time so that they are more effective. She has worked as a trainer at Mastermind.com, which was co-founded by Tony Robbins and Dean Graziosi, where she helped new entrepreneurs on their business journey. She is a speaker at Emotional Intelligence summits on global stages.

Connect with Lynnette here https://thelarochemethod.com

CHAPTER 30

RECLAIMING MY SPIRIT

by Maria E De Lira
https://www.facebook.com/maria.delira.77

Many years had gone by and I had always pushed to get things done my way. I didn't need to be told what I needed to do at home. I saw what needed to be done and went ahead and took care of business. Everything was done in a practical manner.

In 2013, my mother had a stroke while she was visiting my sister in Washington. She ended up in a wheelchair and I became her caregiver. At that time, I had three daughters. One was about to finish high school, another still in high school, and one in middle school.

Juggling my time between doctors' appointments for my mom, the children, and my husband, was taking a toll on me that I didn't even realize. I started to feel tired. Not just tired, but exhausted, to the point that when I would go to bed, I didn't have the energy to get fully on the bed without assistance from my husband. Life went on like this for about 11 months.

I had been asking my siblings for help and my younger sister answered the call. My sister came and took mom up to Washington to give me some time to re-energize. A few months later, my mother had a heart attack and ended up in a coma. Days later, the doctor said her organs were shutting down and we needed to take her off life support. My sister called me to explain what needed to be done. I had to give the okay, as I had full power of attorney. I was trembling and cold as I listened to the doctor ask me If I understood, and to give the okay. I just said "OK." In a matter of moments,

I heard a bunch of noise through the phone line. The only thing I could surmise at that point was they must have been busy unplugging her and we would wait for her organs to shut down. That was one of the hardest decisions that I have ever had to make.

A few days later my sister, who is a nurse, arrived with our dying mother in an RV. Our mother wanted to die at home. The house was filled with relatives who came to pay tribute to my mom and serenade her with her favorite music. This continued for almost a week. On July 22, 2014, our mother gained her wings and was cremated.

I noticed that I was not myself. The woman that was always on the go, was slowly disappearing. I stopped tending to the garden and all my flowers shriveled and died. I felt spiritless. Nothing seemed to engage my attention. I was still doing errands, taking the girls to school, and to their school practices. I didn't want to face the fact that I was depressed and still grieving my mother's death. I felt miserable. I don't remember ever feeling like that.

One day while driving, I don't remember how, I lost control of the vehicle on an overpass. I was going straight to the side and about to hit the concrete side, and for a split second I just let go of the wheel. I just remember thinking, "Oh, my God! I'm gonna die! Please God, just don't let me be mangled. I'd rather die! I don't want to be a burden to my kids! They are too young! Please, just get it over with!"

I prepared for impact and loosened up my body. I remember seeing the street on the bottom of the overpass and just closed my eyes. Suddenly, I felt a force so strong surround my upper body and I couldn't move my arms. They felt like iron and so heavy. I couldn't feel my hands. They felt cold and numb and heavy. I was thinking, "I must be dead," because it was so cold, and I felt so much heavy pressure in my arms and hands. I felt so tired.

I opened my eyes and lo and behold, I was still on the overpass, driving on the right lane. My hands were on the wheel, but I was still cold. The heaviness lasted for about one more minute. My body felt cold, and I started trembling, hands shaking. I was trying to come to terms with what had just happened. I drove to a nearby Walmart® and parked. My body started shaking, my feet felt cold, and I couldn't control my hands. I tried to get my phone, but my hands couldn't hold it. As I was sitting there waiting for my body to recuperate, I felt like I was given a second chance. I was awoken from a nightmare, although it took me days to assimilate what had happened.

I love to read, and during a trip to Barnes and Noble® with one of my daughters, I decided to browse for a book that might catch my attention. I saw the book *Originals: How Non-Conformists Move the World* by Adam Grant. The title caught my eye. I flipped through some pages and the bits and pieces that I read resonated with me. I bought it, took it home and, left it on my desk for a couple of days. When I started reading it, I began to remember my lost self, something sparked inside of me! Something was reignited! A little spark was flickering inside again, and I was feeling warm… at last!

Feelings of hope and reminders of what I had been in my previous years became vivid scenes in my memory. I felt like I was meant to find this book to remind me of plans that I had put on the shelf years ago. My mind became clear, and I started going places again. I began creating impact by nurturing people's souls, seeing their potential, and empowering them to see themselves through a different lens.

I had always felt like a rebel, in a way, trotting through life on my own terms, feeling fear and still doing what needed to be done. I lost it, briefly. This book rekindled my flame and changed everything. This book is for the movers and the shakers movement.

MARIA E DE LIRA

Maria E De Lira is a caring, giving person. She has volunteered for Dress for Success, an organization that provides women with professional attire for job interviews. She also volunteered at The Texas Migrant Council, where they offer early childhood development programs for children and their families. She also volunteered for a local Crisis Hotline, providing support to people in stressful situations.

She has worked as a Health Aide, providing care for the elderly, and worked as an advocate for victims of domestic violence. She enjoys going to the beach, loves spending time in nature, and likes to read. Some of her hobbies are bowling, hunting, and fishing.

Connect with Maria here: https://www.facebook.com/maria.delira.77

CHAPTER 31

UNDERSTANDING ENERGY AND SELF-CARE

by Mary Jackson
Founder, J5 Inc.
http://www.maryejackson.com

Our world is gifted with the richness of words and books that cover a vast array of information in many forms for all of us. It is a blessing to be able to access these easily as opposed to the days of hidden information from long ago. Whatever your need, there is a book written for it. I am an author and lover of books, too, and there are many that have helped me along the way in my life. I also have the privilege of interviewing authors and writers of many different genres and it's been a wonderful experience getting to know authors and what inspires them to write, whether to tell a story, educate, or help others heal.

My favorite books right now are healing and inspirational ones. I do have dog ears in several that are more lighthearted, fantasy, and comical, and I pick those up when I have a few moments in life. I have read *Chicken Soup for the Soul*, *The Four Agreements*, Deepak Chopra's work, all of *Conversations with God*, just to name a few and they have each inspired me on my journey and helped in my growth spiritually and as a woman.

December of 2021 I had no idea heading towards Christmas that I would go through one of the darkest times in my life. My whole family came down with Covid and two days after my son got sick I had to go to the hospital because my heart was skipping and racing non-stop for three days. My calcium and electrolytes were dangerously low as well as having Covid. I was really caught off guard. I have a good diet, take my vitamins, use natural methods as much as possible, and even though I thought I was taking good care of myself, I was burned out.

I was juggling being an author, an advocate for special needs and disabilities, co-hosting two livestream shows, networking, marketing, and the mother of three children. I have been on a spiritual journey for a long time and that never ends; it just continues to grow and change as we do, but nothing had prepared me enough to face the possible end of my life. I was not ready and it was not my time to go. But everything went downhill with my health, and even though my calcium and electrolytes came back up, pneumonia set in. That is one of those symptoms that is feared when a person has Covid. The anti-body shots didn't work and neither did a medication my doctor tried. My life became a constant conversation with God, my angels, helpers, guides, and whomever was out there in the big universe listening. "It is not my time to go. I know this. I have three kids who need me, a husband, a mission, and work to do. You must save me," was my verbal and mental focus.

My faith was challenged, fear looming around at times for what seemed like forever. I asked my daughters to pray over me. One of my daughters told me she could see my light fading as she prayed. That was hard to hear and hard to write in this moment, but it made me pray even harder. Family and friends were praying. I have always believed 100% in the power of prayer. I am an empath and intuitive and do energy work, so every moment that I could I was focusing on sending light and love to the places that needed it in my body.

Finally, I could feel little changes. One step forward and five steps back, but when I was able to read I saw a book on my bedside table. It had sat there forever but called out to me at that time. *Energy Speaks:*

Messages from Spirit on Living, Loving, and Awakening by Lee Harris. I had read parts of it before, but for some reason this time it felt different. The words were yelling at me saying, "You must read this Now." And when something in life speaks to you in this manner, you must listen. And I did.

Energy Speaks helped me understand energy in different ways and how it affects us in our life more than I already understood. There are meditations and tools to apply in your life all the way throughout the book. I now look at my self-care completely different without any guilt for making the space and time I need. And I check in and pay attention to how I am feeling instead of pushing through all of the time to meet a deadline or help 'do one more thing' for my family or someone else. I have learned to prioritize and cut out the things I don't need. Lee Harris gives very easy tools to use for calling back your power if you feel drained, how to feel stronger, forgiveness, releasing guilt, healing relationships with family members, making peace with money, and the art of receiving. Just to name a few.

I am so grateful I 'listened' to that little voice say, "Read this book NOW!" Our inner voice is always there to guide us towards our highest and best good. Learning to actually listen to and take care of ourselves is an ongoing lesson in life. When we have books like *Energy Speaks* to help and guide us on our life journey, we not only get to learn so much more about ourselves and heal or course correct if needed, but we get to learn more about others and the world around us. We are all made of energy and to understand that and how we all connect and interact brings us the opportunity for healing, growth, and a more wonderful life.

Lee Harris helps us understand that giving, receiving, forgiving, loving, and accepting are all forms of energy that help us heal and live the life we truly want.

MARY ELIZABETH JACKSON

Mary Elizabeth Jackson is a two-time #1 Amazon Bestselling author in the collaborative anthologies *The Fearless Entrepreneurs*, and International Bestseller *Invisible No More, Invincible Forever More* (Aug 2021). Jackson is also the 2017 Gold Maxy award-winning author of the children's book series *Perfectly Precious Poohlicious* and *Poohlicious Look at Me* (Tuscany Bay Books), *Poohlicious Oh the Wonder of Me* (Tuscany Bay Books June 2021), and *Cheers from Heaven*, a midgrade reader (Tuscany Bay Books) with co-writer Thornton Cline. Jackson focuses on writing empowering books for kids. Jackson is also a ghostwriter, collaborator, songwriter, educator, and the voice for the Sports2Gether app.

Mrs. Jackson is a special needs advocate and an Ambassador Advocate for AutismTn. Jackson is also an advisor for the Global for profit Billion-Strong. She co-founded and co-hosts Writers Corner Live TV and Special Needs TV Shows that air on Amazon Live, Facebook, Twitter, LinkedIn, and YouTube. Writers Corner Live features author interviews from New York Times bestsellers, International and National bestsellers to multi award winning authors, and all things in the writing world. Special Needs TV features interviews and resources for parents, families, and caregivers. Jackson is also working on an edutainment YouTube channel with her son featuring children's book reviews and family fun and education for all children.

Mrs. Jackson is a very busy mom, wife, empath, and intuitive. She loves nature, being creative, anything funny, and inspiring others to believe in themselves to go from where they are to their full potential. She lives with her hubby, three kids, and dog in the Nashville, Tennessee, area.

"Cherish every moment of life."
~Mary Elizabeth Jackson

You can find Mrs. Jackson's books and other content at www. mary@maryejackson.com.

CHAPTER 32

PICK ANOTHER WAY TO FEEL

by Melissa Walsh
Founder & CEO, MILES Coaching & Consulting, LLC
www.MILEScc.com

I remember when I first learned to read. My family was traveling by car to the Florida Keys for a vacation. I was reading *out loud every* sign and billboard I saw. I was so excited to be able to read! I read the Coppertone billboard, "Fastest tan under the sun!" The next billboard said, "Tan don't burn use Coppertone." I continued reading every advertisement for hotels, how far away the Turtle Hospital was, and how many miles to Key West. My Dad finally couldn't take it anymore and said, quiet in the car! As my parents were on their way to a divorce, I had to constantly devise my own fun.

Reading was fun! Reading opened a world of possibilities for me, a world of a differing perspective. These authors had thoughts and ideas unlike my own. I could read about how the characters in these books felt, and what they thought. These were thoughts which were often insightful and gave me so much more to think about. I could feel what it felt like to be loved, to conquer challenges and the mystery of who done it!

I escaped into the world of books. I read so many. I flew through all the Nancy Drew and Hardy Boys at my grandmother's home. After finishing the "kids" books, I began reading the books my mother and grandmother read and learned about adult things. My grandmother had a book entitled, *You Can If You Think You Can* by Norman Vincent Peale. It seemed interesting. It was a small paperback. Once I started reading, I flew through it, devouring every word.

There were many dramatic, yet heartwarming, stories in this book which helped me understand what it was like to be an adult and think adult things. Do you remember as a child thinking that being an adult would make life so much easier? We now know better! Yet, what I did learn from this book was, we are in ultimate charge of how we react to the things which happen to us in our own lives. I learned how I could make the impossible possible in my own life. I learned things aren't ever as bad as you think they are, and it all begins with a mental shift.

I took these thoughts away with me, and they still drive me today. I understood I could actually pick the way I feel about what is occurring in my life. I get to choose. As a child, I did not feel in control. I couldn't pick what was for dinner, let alone who we saw or where we were going. This book taught me to understand that I, and no one else, could change the way I thought. I found it exciting! This was the one place I was in charge!

Over and over through this book, Mr. Peale reinforces the thought that life is bursting with possibilities, with opportunities we will never see if we keep with a culture of cynicism and distrust.

The very best part of this book is the consistent message of having the right mental attitude and developing the right mental habits resulting in changing your life for the better. He also offers the thought that we have at our access an infinite number of resources. Mr. Peale even suggests methods of application and practical ways of developing mental habits which serve to help you conquer your challenges in life.

I cannot present a more compelling argument than what Norman Vincent Peale did in his book. He dismissed the notion of taking life with a grain of salt. He suggested instead we all choose to take life with a grain of sugar. This helped me understand in my mind it was beneficial to choose the happier thought. I realized the happier thought netted me increased focus and solving the challenge sooner! Thinking cynical thoughts never got me anywhere, and I sure did not get an award for wading through the negativity to get to a solution. It only served to slow me down!

Every time my children came to me with a challenge or conflict, we always started with picking another way to feel, because how they are currently feeling isn't serving to accomplish much. I have told my children this so many times, they tease me and say they will put "Pick Another Way To Feel" on my headstone.

How will you handle the challenges which come your way? You know they will, that's life and life is full of challenges.

Me? I will always come back to the basics I learned in that book.

One. Is the way I feel or think helping me or not? Do I need to pick another way to feel? Do I need to look at another perspective?

Two. I am perfectly capable of handling every challenge which comes my way. Whether I tap in to needed resources, or find a person who can offer advice, I know whatever challenge I am facing, I will get through. I am capable!

Three. In dealing with challenges with other people, I need to know sometimes my way may not be best. Most often, I find the conflicts with others isn't the result of whether the salt should stay in the cupboard or sit out on the table, it is about something else entirely. At this point, I fall back to how do we work this out. Because when you are looking at the big picture, these little things really don't matter.

You can if you think you can!

MELISSA WALSH

Melissa Walsh is the founder, speaker, trainer and coach at MILES Coaching & Consulting and Minnesota Masterminds.

In her years in business, Melissa has developed leaders for success by helping them achieve an amazing work life blend for maximum personal fulfillment. She helps entrepreneurs become high performing leaders and successful business owners. Her wealth of leadership wisdom and experience, coupled with her genuine passion for guiding entrepreneurs, results in true success for her clients. Melissa has fine-tuned the process to help others maximize their skills and heighten their business performance.

She is passionate about igniting the spark in others to learn, grow and reach their highest potential, bringing about a joy-filled life. She believes that when you are living life with passion and on purpose, you will never work another day in your life.

Melissa's superpowers are encouraging to think outside the box challenging the status quo and strategizing successful development of those around her.

Melissa lives in the Twin Cities area in Minnesota.

Connect with Melissa here: www.MILEScc.com

CHAPTER 33

SOMETIMES THE GREATEST ENCOURAGEMENT COMES IN THE SIMPLEST PACKAGES

By Melodie Donovan
Founder, MelodieInc
https://MelodieInc.com

As I started this project, it seemed simple enough… write 1,000 words about a book I read that has inspired me. Honestly, a few years ago the choices would have been fewer to pick from. I've never been much of a reader. But when I do read, it's usually a self-help book. Most people are probably expecting a great John Maxwell or Brené Brown book to be chosen. And I'm sure other authors here have done so and that's great. I struggled to decide which book to write about.

Should I choose *Big Magic* by Elizabeth Gilbert, a Christmas gift I received from my eldest son? It was a fascinating book about how an idea is born, among other things. It pushed me to think a little differently. I am more open to the creative process for having read it.

Another book, *Make Your Bed* by Admiral William H. McRaven, was based off a commencement speech he gave at a college graduation. By making your bed each day you set yourself up with a successful day each day because you already accomplished one task. It's a quick read. He has a lot of other great nuggets included as well. *Make Your Bed* made me feel like I can set goals and achieve them by comparing the goals to the simple task of making my bed.

However, I kept coming back to one book. I thought to myself, "Surely, I can't write about this book." But I felt very compelled that this was the book. Sometimes it is the simplest of things that make the biggest impact. He's a well-known author. He is popular to young and old alike. He's a best-selling author many times over. The author is Dr. Seuss. And the book is *Oh, the Places You'll Go!* What a fantastically encouraging book.

My first encounter with the book was as it was read at my son's kindergarten graduation ceremony, May 2000. I've read the book countless times since. And I have given it as a high school graduation gift many times over. I love the book because it encourages you… "You have brains in your head" … "You can steer yourself any direction you choose." "You'll be on your way up. See the great sights"… "You will be best of the best. Wherever you go you'll top all the rest. Except when you don't."

It includes realism that life will have its challenges. Even then, it encourages you to hang in there, to work out of your "slump." It is written for children by a children's author. But maybe it wasn't. Usually, the best things comes in small boxes or in this case the simplest of books. "Life is a great balancing act." "You will move mountains." "You're off to great places."

If you haven't read it, you should! It is a quick read. It's more than just a few motivational sayings, but it's shorter than a 200- to 250-page self-help book. It's a win-win!!

Now the big question… How did it transform my life?

As I sat in the audience hearing it read to my son and his young classmates, I thought she was reading it to me as well. I always felt like I didn't get much encouragement in my house growing up. Some children are fortunate to have parents who believe in them and help their children dream. But my parents weren't like that. I did have a mentor, Mike. I called him my church dad. He was the one that walked beside me and encouraged me to work hard, get good grades so I could be accepted into college. As the years passed, we drifted apart. *Oh, the Places You'll Go* encouraged me to be the parent for my children that I didn't have. And to be the Encourager to others if they needed one. And yes, it was the Encourager I needed when I was struggling with my career goals and doubting myself. I've given several copies of the book to others over the years and I keep a copy on my bookshelf to come back and re-read occasionally. I encourage you now to check it out from the library or purchase a copy for your personal library. Read it. Be encouraged to dream of whatever you want your life to be. No matter your age. Then do it!! Happy reading. ☺

MELODIE DONOVAN

Melodie Donovan is an Award-Winning #1 International Bestselling Author, an IT Professional of 20 years, a bartender for 6, and a serial entrepreneur for 11. Melodie launched her financial coaching business to help women with their journey to financial freedom. She is a Certified Financial Coach through Ramsey Financial Coaching. She became a travel agent and Traveling Vineyards wine guide to learn more about wine, meet other people, and enjoy some wine along the way.

Melodie is thankful for everyone who has encouraged her over the years. She is especially thankful for her children, Zach and Casey. By encouraging her children that they can be anything they want to be with a little hard work, a lot of faith and belief in themselves she has learned to be kinder to herself and an encourager to herself and others.

She is thankful to have another opportunity to contribute to another Action Takers Publishing book.

You can connect with Melodie here: https://MelodieInc.com.

CHAPTER 34

OUTWITTING MYSELF FROM LIMITING BELIEFS AND OBSTACLES

by Mistie Layne

*Empowerment and Resiliency Expert, Step Up
and Speak Out*

www.stepupandspeakout.com

Certainly, I am not alone in pondering the question "who am I" and "what do I really want in life." After surviving, at the time, seemingly unbearable adversity, my life started taking on new direction and purpose. I knew I was changed, but had no idea what the changes meant, how they would affect my legacy, or how to even feel about it. As circumstance allowed, I was handed a copy of *Outwitting the Devil: The Secret to Freedom and Success* by Napoleon Hill and I entered a new dimension of thinking, understanding, and reasoning as I shifted into a newfound mindset with intrigue.

After going from medical school to facing a forty-year prison sentence for killing somebody in an accident behind my horrific ten-year cocaine addiction, I was tormented by survivor's guilt, shame, fear and loss of personal identity. Although my life was spared through all the hell I survived, I was hardly "alive." Writing my life story while in a grim jail cell was the therapy that saved my life, but I was too ashamed or afraid of the judgment to publish my story once I was released from prison. I knew God intended to use my voice, but didn't know how to find the courage to STEP UP AND SPEAK OUT with transparency until I read Hill's book. Through being open minded to his teachings of positivity, gratitude, drifting and the art of living, I discovered my limitations around fear were created in my own mind and that defeat is temporary and success comes right after defeat if we continue our path. I understood I needed to act by using my faith as fear instead of withdrawing. To achieve success (of freedom), we must transform our fear into the very faith that will become our fuel. I was too stuck in allowing my past to rob my future to clearly see what my limiting beliefs were and how they were preventing me from becoming true to myself and facing my own demons.

This book moved me into profoundly realizing my true potential as a human being and allowed me the freedom to be my authentic self I found after a self-discovery journey of reality. A new mindset I had never entertained of "taking control of my own will and destiny" evolved and I began to feel powerful over the voices of doubt and self-sabotage in my head. Once I took accountability for my actions and forgave myself, I was then able to push doubt, fear, limitations, negative thoughts, and shame to the side to allow the space to fill with love, happiness, good health and successful living. I gave myself the space and time to work through my trauma, realize the lessons from it, and recognize myself as an authority on all I had survived.

Outwitting the devil is a metaphor and the devil can be anything we imagine it to be. For me, it was about outwitting myself by learning to own up to my faults, let go of my transgressions, and allowing forgiveness of myself and others to happen. Additionally, it was outwitting myself from doubt and fear, even fear of success! I had always thought achievement was measured by tangible possessions and never understood the practical understandable philosophy of achievement Hill taught me. Success for me now is blocking out the "drifting" my mind slips into and refraining from the negative conforms our society is so accustomed to. Success means being able

THE BOOK I READ

to speak honestly and passionately about drug addiction, domestic abuse, perfectionism and people pleasing to make a difference in the world for others. Success means focusing on what I want to achieve and the type of legacy I want to leave behind and not derailing from that course, no matter the negative forces around me. Success means finding the courage to transparently share my story to bring education and awareness to the world so we can JUDGE less and MENTOR more. Success is allowing my story today to save a life tomorrow. I discovered the power behind transparency from the wisdom and knowledge of this advanced book of poetic reasoning and mind-shifting. No longer do I allow my mind to "drift" and open the door of doubt. Instead, I use Hill's defined habits to outwit my devil; 1) I seek definite purpose in life, 2) I am obtaining self-mastery, 3) I use my adversity as benefits to teach others, 4) I use time as my tool, 5) I find peace and harmony, despite the noise in my head. To prevent "drifting," I do my own thinking, create a definite plan for my purpose, I extract a seed of benefit from every temporary defeat, I accept my greatest asset is time and strive to better protect my time, I remind myself that fear is a filler that occupies the parts of my mind the "devil" likes to fill. I operate from a state of mind that can instead be filled with what I want, and what I now know I CAN get!

I may not have fully unlocked the secret to freedom and success, but I now know the definitions of freedom and success and what they mean to me in this lifetime. I understand how powerful "persuasion" can be and how "drifting" opens the door for all things bad! We are created with emotion, empathy and compassion for a reason, and I now understand how using my adversity can help ease suffering of others by teaching them to avoid the forest of shame, suffocating under guilt, or drowning in a river of sorrow and self-pity. It is no longer about us, but about the people we can help despite our past decisions or shortcomings.

We may never fully tap our own true potential, but I am now fueled by faith in believing it is obtainable and achievable. During my drug addiction, I felt my soul was tormented daily by my own demon inside, my own critical voice of destruction. I silence the voice by taking accountability and allowing forgiveness. With my new courage and confidence, I discovered the liberation and freedom that comes with transparency and pray you learn to outwit your devil, too. Unlock your success and freedom by understanding the dynamics of your own mind. Be your own hero; set yourself free!

MISTIE LAYNE

Mistie Layne went from being a Texas beauty queen at the brink of becoming a surgeon to facing a forty-year prison sentence. Cocaine and domestic abuse robbed her of 10 years of life and led to a horrific rock bottom she courageously describes in her best-selling book, *What Goes Up*.

After hiding her dark ugly secrets for years, she now STEPS UP AND SPEAKS OUT with passion and transparency about how to overcome your worst to live your best. She now transforms lives by helping others release toxic beliefs through transparency and resilience.

Mistie's talk show, Dare 2 Share, provides a platform for TRANSPARENCY to evolve and freedom to emerge.

She can help you Step Up and Speak Out by instilling confidence to face your truth and courage to speak out, allowing your story today to save a life tomorrow. She also inspires resiliency through her Write 2 Ignite Women's Empowerment Retreats … Speak Out Public Speaking Workshops … and in her collaborative book, *Action Takers Who Step Up and Speak Out*.

Mistie is the co-founder of Tween Esteem, which is a camp for 9- to 12-year-old girls to learn about self-esteem and empowerment. She also practices Nuclear Medicine full-time, serving as a frontline healthcare worker, was awarded Overall Global Achiever of 2021, nominated Woman of the Year, and is a contributing journalist for several international magazines.

Connect with Mistie here: www.stepupandspeakout.com

CHAPTER 35

CONNECTING – FINDING MY TRUTH ON A BOOKSHELF

by Nancy Lockhart
Founder, Lockhart Marketing
www.lockhart-marketing.com

I had always found it hard to believe that a book could really change someone's life. As a young girl I was an avid reader. I loved *Little House on the Prairie* and Judy Blume books. They helped me to see life through someone else's eyes, have adventure, or feel that I was not alone in whatever drama I was living out in my young life. But it was a stretch to think that a book could actually change a core belief of mine or rock the foundation of how I was raised, but *Conversations with God* by Neale Donald Walsch certainly did that.

I was raised Catholic, went to Catholic school, got married in a Catholic Church. I participated in all of the Sacraments. Up to that point in my life it all made sense. I was given the rules and I worked to follow them, and if I made a mistake I went to confession.

In 1989 I got married. In 1993 I was divorced. My ideas about marriage were challenged and changed. My divorce was never something that I would have thought would happen to me, yet I was the one who ended my marriage. I had begun to question other foundational areas of my life, including my religion and my relationship with God.

My good friend invited me to the Bodhi Tree, a spiritual bookstore on Melrose Avenue in Los Angeles, California. The title *Conversations with God* caught my attention. How interesting that the author believed that he had a whole book worth of conversations with God. Why was he so special? I pulled the book off of the shelf and read the excerpt on the back –

"I have heard the crying of your heart. I have seen the search of your soul. I know how deeply you have desired the truth. In pain have you called out for it, and in joy. Unending have you beseeched Me. Show Myself. Explain Myself. Reveal Myself."

I bought the book.

I started by approaching the book as a fantasy, a made-up dialogue I would have loved to have had. I was hoping to discover questions that I may not have thought to ask and that may help me align new beliefs or challenge my assumptions from the author's point of view. I had experienced a similar concept on the radio, where the host of the show puts himself in the role of Jesus Christ, even requiring questions be addressed to Jesus and the host responded to questions that listeners had about all kinds of life situations as if he was the Son of God. I found it very entertaining and thought provoking; however, it felt very theological, very church-like–come to the master to determine your fate according to the Gospel, understand that rules must be followed or there's no getting into heaven.

Reading *Conversations with God* was a much different experience. The conversation was authentic, the questions were honest, and the responses were thoughtful, loving, forthright and NOT judgmental at all.

Neale Donald Walsch seemed like a very regular person who had experienced real life. He wasn't an exalted profit, or a noble cleric. He is a radio guy. He had been married and divorced several times. He experienced homelessness for a year. He got mad at God at one of the lowest points in his life and wanted answers. In his mind, he received those answers from God and wrote them down.

I really don't care how the words came, or if they came from GOD. Some people might think that I should. For some people this book could be seen as scary and blasphemous. In my mind and what is constantly reinforced throughout the book, is that the words are meant to be used as they resonate with you. Dismiss what doesn't make sense, what doesn't ring true in your soul. The book will either help you to think differently or reinforce the beliefs that you hold dear. I promise it will make you feel.

Once I read the first book, I was hungry for more. So many of the questions that I had, based on my religious beliefs, were resolved with the learnings in this book. The God that resonated with me was the God that spoke in this book.

After I read *Conversations with God,* I read the second and third books with the same title and began exploring my spirituality on a deeper level. I began to read other books that explored a different approach to my relationship with what or who I called "God."

I discovered Law of Attraction and the Quantum Success Coaching Academy with Christy Whitman and became a certified Law of Attraction Life Coach. The teaching I learned through my training aligned with my initial discovery and the joy that I found in *Conversations with God.* I leveraged my law of attraction learnings and my background in marketing to launch my own marketing organization, Lockhart Marketing, where my tagline is "Unlock the Heart of Your Business."

I believe that discovering *Conversations with God* and Neal Donald Walsch significantly changed my relationship with my higher self. It allowed me to build a confidence and a "knowing" about what my life is meant to be and how I can do my part to bring the conversation, wisdom, and overall hope to the people that I work with and live with in my everyday life.

This book truly changed the way I thought about life, humanity, what it means to be good and why we are here at this point in time.

I believe that life is meant to be an experience. I believe that we are meant to have contrast so that we can evolve and grow. I believe that we are all blessed and sacred no matter what religions, beliefs, or non-beliefs we practice. And I believe that we were and will continue to embrace the love of God through eternity.

In my heart I know that I was meant to discover this book and experience the deep connection to a wisdom and guidance that I had needed but wasn't sure how to find or where to look. *Conversations with God* opened my eyes, and I am forever changed.

NANCY LOCKHART

Nancy is the Founder of Lockhart Marketing, Certified Law of Attraction Life Coach, Executive Advisor at University of California – Santa Barbara, Customer Experience Program, #1 International Bestselling Author of *Invisible No More; Invincible Forever More* and Podcast/Livestream host of the "Beyond the Logo" show.

Connect with Nancy here: www.lockhart-marketing.com

CHAPTER 36

FROM SHEEP TO SHEPHERD

by Paige Davidson
Founder, Fasting with Paige
www.fastingwithpaige.com

I am embarrassed now to admit it, but I used to be such a sheep! From a medical consumer perspective, that is.

Allow me to explain. My parents were raised in the hills of Eastern Kentucky, a poor, rural area where doctors were revered above all other professions. A doctor was the most educated professional in the community, and the most respected. Neither of my parents would ever consider going to a doctor's appointment dressed in anything but their Sunday finest. The doctor's word was gospel; there was no debate or second-guessing a doctor. You did what the doctor said, period. You accepted any diagnosis as final, end of story.

This is the environment that I was raised in, even though my family left the hills behind when I was three to move to an urban center of the state. Although my thinking wasn't quite as black and white as my parents' was where it concerned doctors, this little apple didn't fall too far from the tree. I did, and still do, have a great deal of respect for doctors. I differed from my parents, however, in realizing that not every single doctor was the consummate, learned professional who knew all. Every profession has large numbers of excellent practitioners, a few mediocre ones, and a few bad apples, physicians included. Still, overall, I had a very healthy respect for doctors and did consider them the professional, the one in charge of my health, and very trustworthy. I did not doubt that they knew what they needed to know to provide me with excellent and accurate medical care. That is, until I read the book *Lies My Doctor Told Me: Medical Myths That Can Harm Your Health*, by Ken D. Berry, MD, FAAFP.

I happened across this book as I cruised Amazon looking for a great new read. At first glance, this was not the book I was searching for! *Lies My Doctor Told Me* – what? How controversial, how inflammatory, who would write such a book? Dr. Ken Berry, apparently. This was the first surprise, that a medical doctor had written a book with such an outrageous title. But then, I read the subtitle: *Medical Myths That Can Harm Your Health*. Now THIS got my attention. The title of this book both repelled and intrigued me. I purchased it and began reading immediately. I have never had more "light bulb" moments while reading a book as I did as I devoured this volume. Who wouldn't be fascinated by a book whose first chapter title was "Trust in God, Not Your Doctor"?

Aha moment number one: the ultimate purpose of this book was to teach me, as a patient, to do my own thinking. Not that I am not a thinking person, but isn't it a doctor's job, having attended medical school and learned everything they needed to know to advise me in caring for my health? Isn't the doctor supposed to be in charge, the educated professional with medical knowledge that I wouldn't even begin to know about? Well, apparently not!

Aha moment number two: I am fully in charge of my own health. Sure, I had taken steps in this direction in recent years. After 40+ years of yo-yo dieting, gaining my way up to 315 pounds, and losing but not maintaining a 150-pound weight loss through weight loss surgery, I discovered intermittent fasting. I adopted this healthy lifestyle, lost 110 pounds, healed several health conditions, wrote several books, was featured on the cover of Woman's World magazine, became a certified health coach focusing on intermittent fasting and mindset coaching, and along the way became empowered to truly make healthy decisions for myself. But when it comes to overseeing my own overall healthcare instead of doctors? How am I supposed to know, from a wealth of medical information in which I have no training or expertise, how to heal myself, I wondered as I read this ground-breaking book. Who knew the extent to which my food, dietary, and lifestyle choices affect my health and well-being, beyond just my BMI? What a revelation to learn how my health is both robust and fragile at the same time. That if my own personal diet and lifestyle choices are correct, that I almost can't get sick; and if they are incorrect, that I almost can't get well.

Aha moment number three was an especially big one, that I must be a partner with my physician/medical team, not simply a sheep who blindly follows directions and advice without listening to my own intuition and asking thoughtful questions. I quickly learned that my doctor's role in our relationship was to remain as up-to-date on current research, and not to blindly believe every word that comes out of big-pharma sponsored research, or the adorable drug-rep's mouth. I learned that my role was to stop being mentally and physically lazy! To stop blindly trusting my doctor and big-pharma to give me a magic pill or some magic treatment to solve health problems caused by actions that are likely within my control. Clearly, I was going to have to start thinking about my own holistic health, research the latest options, consider solutions, and ask my doctor well-researched questions, in a respectful way. To truly become a partner in my own health care.

And finally, as I read, I came to understand how critical my doctor's interest in my own personal research, questions, and suggestions was. If my doctor does not realize that these actions are those of a patient who is engaged and invested in their own medical care, if my doctor is insulted by these actions, if my doctor expects me to accept their word as final without questioning it, then it is time to find a new doctor who WILL respect and encourage my role as a partner in our relationship.

Lies My Doctor Told Me is a must read. Because of this single book, I went from being a sheep, blindly following every doctor's order while ignoring my own thoughts and intuition, to literally becoming the shepherd of my own healthcare, guiding and directing a team of healthcare professionals in a collaborative relationship with me, to provide the best care possible for me as their unique patient.

Through this book, Dr. Berry will convince you that you should never trust something so precious and valuable as your own health to the opinion of a single person – not even your doctor.

PAIGE DAVIDSON

Physically, emotionally, and spiritually exhausted after a lifetime of yo-yo dieting, Paige Davidson began a journey in search of something different - true healing. Her unique journey began with Christian counseling, and the discovery of intermittent fasting, a healthy method of alternating eating food within a period of time, with clean fasting, on a daily basis.

Paige has lost an astounding 176 pounds, healed several health conditions, was featured in Woman's World magazine in 2020 and in 2021 (she also appeared on the cover in 2020) and wrote a workbook, *Fast With Paige: Health & Healing Practices for Forever Freedom*.

Additionally, as an intermittent fasting expert and an international #1 best-selling author, Paige has been a special guest on over a dozen podcasts, as well as two Summits.

This spiritual journey with physical healing led Paige to a deep calling to help as many women like her as possible. She is a certified health coach specializing in intermittent fasting and mindset work, providing virtual coaching for clients globally (www.fastingwithpaige. com). She has coached, inspired, and mentored thousands of intermittent fasters virtually throughout the world.

Connect with Paige at www.fastingwithpaige.com.

CHAPTER 37

OPEN DOOR SEASON

by Prophetess Nalo Thomas Mitchell
President and Founder, NWPNM, Nuggets With
Prophetess Nalo Ministries
facebook.com/ProphetessNalo

It was a privilege to attend Arizona State University where I majored in Broadcast Journalism. The campus was absolutely gorgeous and reminded me of paradise. My major opened up so many doors, but I was too young to appreciate the "Open Door Season" that was taking place in my life.

I had an internship at a major radio station in Chicago, Illinois, and television station in Phoenix, Arizona. My desire was to become a radio personality. But it took several years for me to complete my undergraduate degree and it seemed as if my dream to go into broadcast journalism would never come to fruition.

I worked for several employers in my 20s and never really found my jam. My identity and thought process was to help take care of my children as a divorcé and single parent. One day, I decided to leave Corporate America and work in the nonprofit sector. I took a major pay cut, but the rewards and dividends of pouring into the others far exceeded any financial compensation.

Fate had its way and I married my husband, best friend, and soulmate Elder Darrell Mitchell. Our union meant that I had someone to share life and love with and no longer had to carry the brunt of all the financial, mental, and emotional responsibilities alone. Decades later while working in the nonprofit sector I was asked to transition to a new position and was esteemed to begin working in a new department. It was a tumultuous time in my career. A major transition had taken place in the organization in which I was employed, and I found myself stressed, uptight, and things just weren't right. However, quitting was not an option.

During the season of transition in my career, work had become so overwhelming between the phone calls, emails, special requests and orders that everything began moving at lightning speed. There was nothing I could do to control the pace. Executing the tasks that were set before me on a day-to-day basis began to wear on me.

Discouraged and carrying the stress from work to home wasn't a pleasant experience. I became desperate for permanent change and sought strategies that would allow me to create balance in my life. It was "Open Door Season" for me, but that did not come without challenge.

Yet, I had another issue. In the midst of the transition, I began to believe that I was ill-equipped to handle the task at hand. Then I remembered "I can do all things [which The Lord has called me to do] through Him who strengthens *and* empowers me [to fulfill His purpose]." There was yet Kingdom Purpose in the laborious times, but I just couldn't see it.

I realized that I was trying to handle everything with my own strength. It was then that I had an aha moment and understood that I needed more prayer to catapult me through that particular season of difficulty. Prayer became the catalyst and chain breaker of bondage that had been holding me captive.

I sought the advice of a family member who had a successful career. There were organizational skills and balance that I needed in order to set my career ablaze and be the successful beacon of light that I was purposed to be. I was advised to think of my career in the same manner as an air traffic controller. "Bring in the airplanes that need to come in first," in other words I had to learn how to prioritize. This reprioritization was a monumental shift and things began to fall into place.

I heard about a book that would change my life forever. *The Checklist Manifesto: How to Get Things Right* by Atul Gawande. The book contained the necessary nuggets I needed to organize my tasks and get things done.

Increasing my capacity to learn new techniques and strategies would become my saving grace by doing something simple, creating a 'Checklist.' The checklist allowed me to be strategic, less stressed, and realize that I would no longer be tormented by the stress that weighed me down in former seasons. It also allowed me to discover my strengths, experience more joy, and use new methodologies with purpose "on purpose" each day.

Checklist Manifesto allowed me to see myself as a repairer of the breach and a developer of others as a positive thinker. I developed a game plan and finished the job in a Spirit of Excellence. My life transcended more meaningfully because I learned the importance of balance. My career became more enjoyable and carrying the stress home to my family became a thing of the past. My life became more meaningful because I learned the importance of balance. Each day I would write a daily checklist regarding the expectations and tasks set before me.

In your "Open Door Season," you will experience obstacles that are often referred to as mountain tops and valleys.

However, you must remember to create an atmosphere that allows for openness, grace, and steadiness because life will happen.

When life gives us lemons, I believe it's pivotal to:

- Make lemonade that suits your fancy
- Create a balance between the sweet and sour

- Say a prayer, journal and look to mentors and experts who can help to catapult you to the next level
- Write a checklist
- Determine the heavenly strategies you need in order to win in life
- Pray until something happens
- Press into the goal, lean and walk in your purpose on purpose
- Push until the right door opens on your behalf

Remember, storms happen in life. The storm may consist of a challenging season in your career, the loss of a loved one, a physical or emotional storm. But, keep moving because better days are ahead. Keep walking up the mountainside until you're able to look down and see the valley, get a new perspective, dream again, believe again, and press into your "Open Door Season" of overflow.

PROPHETESS NALO THOMAS MITCHELL

Prophetess Nalo Thomas Mitchell is the wife of Elder Darrell Mitchell. They met at a church service in Springfield, Illinois over 15 years ago and have been married with Christ as the head of their lives for more than 11 years. This anointed Woman of God believes in empowering and encouraging others to reach their Kingdom purpose. She is a born again believer who gave her life to Christ in January 1996. She believes that when you are steadfast before The Lord, you'll learn that you are an amazing masterpiece, born in the right place at the right time!

Prophetess Nalo is a published author in the #1 International Bestselling book, *Wellness for Winners.* Earning a Bachelor of Arts in Broadcasting from the Walter Cronkite School of Journalism at Arizona State University in 2007. She went on to further her education and obtained a Masters Degree in Organizational Leadership and Change from Colorado Technical University in 2013. Prophetess Nalo was honored to become an ordained Prophetess of the gospel in 2017 under the leadership of Table of Life Ministries and an ordained Pastor in 2021 at Faith Community Center both in Springfield, IL. where both she and her husband have served in ministry.

Prophetess Nalo is the Founder and President of NWPNM, Nuggets With Prophetess Nalo Ministries. NWPNM is a not-for-profit organization created for charitable and educational purposes to empower others while sharing the gospel.

Connect with Nalo here: facebook.com/ProphetessNalo.

CHAPTER 38

THE TRUTH ABOUT HAPPINESS

by Rebecca L. Norrington
Happiness Specialist & Inner Peace Practitioner
https://rebeccanorrington.com

Do you remember blowing out candles on your birthday cake or throwing coins into a fountain and making a wish? When I was younger, I always wished for the same two things. I wanted to live to my potential, and I wanted to be happy. Like most, I thought I'd be happy when;

-- I found Mr. Right (I found him, then I lost him in a divorce)
-- I had more money than I was able to spend
-- New York Times Best Selling Author
-- Oprah Winfrey produces my live TV show *RealitySpirituality: The Truth About Happiness*

Yes, in the '80s, it *looked* like I had it all. I married, bought a house, traveled a lot, and birthed a brilliant son. But, I was never satisfied—I wasn't happy. I began to look for someone or something to blame. At first, I thought it was my husband's fault. Then I *knew* it was my husband's fault. Eventually, I got the bad news and discovered happiness is *my* responsibility. Damn it. Since happiness was what I'd wished for all my life, I began seeking, with laser focus, was it possible to be happy all the time? I made a personal commitment to finding out.

I read countless self-help books, attended seminars, workshops, and weekend retreats when I started the search. I concluded that I wasn't happy because I didn't have a purpose, so I spent a decade searching for it. Why am I here? What gifts do I have to share? What am I passionate about? I knew I'd find *lasting* happiness when I found my purpose. Wrong. The happiness I sought was only accessed by *being*, not doing.

Power vs. Force: The Hidden Determinants of Human Behavior, written by David R. Hawkins, M.D., Ph.D., changed my life. In *Power vs. Force*, Dr. Hawkins focuses on calculating the energy levels of human consciousness. According to Hawkins, all energy levels of human consciousness below 200 are destructive of life in both the individual and society. All levels above 200 are expressions of power. Hawkins states, 200 is the point that divides the areas of force (or **falsehood**) from power (or **truth**). The book provides detailed descriptions of each energy level, and it's worth the read.

Levels of Human Consciousness

Shame	20	Courage	200
Guilt	30	Neutrality	250
Apathy	50	Willingness	310
Grief	75	Acceptance	350
Fear	100	Reason	400
Desire	125	Love	500
Anger	150	Joy	540
Pride	175	Peace	600
		Enlightenment	700-1000

Power vs. Force exposed the truth. I was living most of my life in lower states of consciousness. My conscious energy levels were stuck in shame, desire, anger, and pride.

Shame

Two occasions in my life have caused me decades of shame. First, in the second grade, I told my mother that my teacher didn't know I was adopted. My mother's response sent me spiraling into a life of shame that lasted 20 years. She screamed, "You're not supposed to tell anyone you're adopted—it's a secret." And for 20 years, I lied to keep the awful, repulsive, and horrible secret—I was adopted. But that wasn't enough shame for me. No, I added to my shame when I began making up lies to *support* the shame. Example: I'd hear, "You don't look like your mother or father," and my reply was, "I know, I look like my grandmother."

Shame Now

I can't find it.

*The second example of shame that lived with me for *four decades* will be shared in another book.

Anger

I LOVED getting angry. Anger made me *feel powerful*. I was addicted. I used anger to control the people I *claimed* to love and intimidate people I didn't know. I thought barking, threatening, and demanding what I wanted in a high-pitched voice was proper and acceptable behavior. It was my way or the highway. I *loved* it. I *wanted* people to fear me because I thought that was a powerful position. However, after reading *Power vs. Force*, I realized that anger is just another form of drama, and both are extremely low energetic levels of consciousness.

Yes, anger used to make me *feel* powerful, but all anger comes from a place of weakness. It took me decades to realize and admit that truth.

Anger Now

Fast forward to October 29, 2018, when my mother died. After my mother's death, I found out she gifted the family home worth $330,000 and its contents to her handyman. (My mother was diagnosed with early dementia in 2007 and lacked mental capacity when legal documents were signed.)

It's 2022, and I'm in a battle with the attorney responsible for drafting the documents gifting the family house to the handyman. Oh, and are you ready for the plot to thicken in this crazy twisted story? The attorney responsible for drafting the document gifting the family home to the handyman drafted another document *removing* me as Successor Trustee by appointing <u>himself</u> Successor Trustee over my family's estate. The document removing me as Successor Trustee is not notary stamped to add insult to injury!

My purpose for sharing this is two-fold. Presently, it's rare for me to get angry now because of four decades of what I practice. However, in 2018, I was able to <u>laugh out loud</u> two weeks after (not before) finding out the house was going to my mother's handyman.

The Truth

-- I was attached to that house.
-- I had expectations.
-- I took what happened with the house personally.
-- I blamed my mother.
-- I lacked trust that the Universe was serving me.

Attachments, expectations, taking anything personally, blame, and a lack of trust subtract from happiness.

Spiritually speaking, neither the attorney, handyman, nor my mother was responsible for what happened. The Universe choreographed it all for my betterment—to grow, expand, transcend, and transform my consciousness. In 2022, my *conscious* energy levels remain rooted in acceptance, peace, courage, reason, and love. And, the person I used to be doesn't exist anymore.

Happiness is a practiced skill. ~rln

REBECCA L. NORRINGTON

Rebecca L. Norrington is a Happiness Specialist and an Inner Peace Practitioner. She's a student of the Universe and Its Laws. She holds a Bachelor of Science Degree in Psychology and decades of education and training on topics from Spirituality to Human Behavior. Her professional journey includes several vocations: Speaker, Podcast Host, Author, Spiritual Teacher, Workshop and Retreat Facilitator, Fitness Instructor & Reiki Practitioner.

In 2012, Rebecca began hosting *RealitySpirituality: The Truth About Happiness* on BlogTalkRadio heard every Sunday at 9am Pacific time.

In 2015, Rebecca developed an eight-week course, The Truth About Happiness. She's instructed classes in California, Oregon, and coming soon to Nevada.

Rebecca has been an AFAA Certified Fitness Instructor for over four decades. She specializes in in-person and online classes, including Tone2theBone, Aqua BootCamp, Foam Rolling, Chair Aerobics, Chair Stretch, Dynamic Stretch, Balance & Breathing, and Facersize.

Rebecca's first book, *RealitySpirituality; The Truth About Happiness*, was published in 2014 and can be purchased on Amazon. Her second book, *Programmed for Unhappiness*, will be published in Spring 2022.

Rebecca realizes, while prioritizing happiness above all other conditions might be a radical message, people discover that all aspects of their lives automatically shift when they make happiness a number-one commitment. ~rln

Happiness is defined as the ability to be at peace regardless of what happens and what doesn't happen. ~rln

Connect with Rebecca here: https://rebeccanorrington.com

CHAPTER 39

THE BOOK THAT FUELED ME TO MEDITATE CONSISTENTLY

by Rita Farruggia
Founder and CEO of Happybeingwell.com
www.HappyBeingWell.com

Reading Dr. Joe Dispenza's book *Breaking the Habit of Being Your-self* allowed me to further understand the relationship between the body and the mind. This book was the catalyst for me to take a deep dive into how our body stores all of our emotions and memories, which influences the type of chemicals the body will send to the brain when you try to change your thoughts in order to change your actions. This was the catalyst for me to start paying attention to what my body was doing and feeling throughout my day to tune into my inner self to expand my consciousness of myself. Throughout the day, I stop to check in to sense if my muscles are tense or relaxed, the pace of my heart rate (fast or slow), and where am I breathing from - my belly or chest. If my muscles are tense, then this prompts me to do a quick ten-minute meditation to reset myself to focus on truth. Meaning, throughout our daily lives we each experience some stress. For example, our computer freezes, we are stuck in traffic, etc.

Reading this book made me realize the importance of being aware of our physical bodies and to ensure we don't allow our physical bodies to get addicted to being in a stressed physiology. My goal is to ensure I pull myself out of a physiological stress response through awareness of how both my body and mind react to a stressful event and pull myself out of it. Through self-massage, shifting my thoughts to "how can I leverage the time of being stuck in traffic?" Framing questions like this, prompts me to put on a Tony Robbins audio training or catch up on one of my favorite podcasts. Now I am using this time to learn more and reinforce good habits instead of living in a state of frustration.

Motivated Me to Stay Consistent in My Meditation Practice

The more we learn about the benefits and results of a particular activity, the more motivated we are towards taking action towards it. Meditating consistently while participating in society is challenging for anyone due to the demands and pressures of our everyday life. In addition, it is an unfamiliar activity to us because since we were school kids, we have been conditioned to live from our conscious minds (beta) to learn and accomplish things. We were never taught in our societal institutions to quiet our mind and sit still to not think thoughts. Our minds are used to always thinking during the day whether you are aware of it or not. In fact, according to scientists, we think 60,000 thoughts a day. Our thoughts and feelings influence the same state of being, which creates the same behaviors and keeps you stuck on recreating the same reality.

When we are different in terms of our responses (from negative to positive) to life events, then we will be a match to a potential reality we want to create. Through the practice of daily meditation, we can observe our mind and body then stop thinking to feel inner peace within ourselves so our body and mind develop a habit of feeling this so you can more easily anchor yourself to a peaceful state of clarity instead of a stressed state of confusion. Living from a state of confusion allows you to be easily distracted by various external stimuli preventing you from taking focused action to create the reality you want to experience.

Also, Dr. Dispenza discusses in this book that we are also changing our energy which we put out into the electromagnetic field. The energy we emit is what we will be pulled toward, that potential reality, or it will find us. Also, this book highlights how change requires both our thoughts and feelings to be aligned. When we think about what we want and also feel it in our heart, then we are sending coherent waves out like a laser, making us powerful creators of the life we want to create and experience. We also need to have belief that the outcomes we desire that we can visualize in our minds and desire with our hearts will manifest. This motivated me to create two free e-books for others to download. The first one is how to meditate easily when first starting and staying consistent. It is called, "Meditation Made Easy E-Guide" and can be downloaded at www.Happybeingwell.com under the Blog Section on the Resources web page. The second e-book to download for free is, "Overcome Limiting Beliefs," which can also be found on www. Happybeingwell.com in the dropdown menu of the blog section in the Resources web page. You can also listen to free guided meditations on the Happy Being Well podcast on Apple iTunes or Spotify.

This book, *Breaking the Habit of Being Yourself*, along with other books, seminars and courses are the fuel for me to commit to living a mindfulness lifestyle where it has become a habit that allows me to focus on devoting my energy towards progress. This book is effective in explaining all the necessary steps needed to create a new mind. It also highlights real life examples of people who use visualization meditations to manifest their visions into reality including Dr. Joe Dispenza's daughter who for 30 days consistently visualized working in Italy for the summer before manifesting into reality a summer job in Italy. This is one of the reasons why I developed www.Happybeingwell. com, a wellness e-commerce website to provide people with wellness products and meditative tools to support living a mindfulness lifestyle so they can live to their fullest potential, contribute to society, and inspire others to do the same so they can be happy being well.

RITA FARRUGGIA

Rita Farruggia is a self-care/self-love/happiness expert. Rita is the founder & CEO of happybeingwell.com, which is a wellness e-commerce site devoted to providing organic self-care products to amplify your wellness so you can be happy being well.

HappyBeingWell.com has a mission of being the #1 Self-Care Community in North America.

Rita's mission is to awaken people to their love, teaching them how to reprogram their subconscious to align with truth through creating a daily self-care practice. It is through a commitment to a daily self-care practice that we can eliminate the noise of the world, stress, anxiety and our rapid thoughts. This allows us to be able to align with our personal truth, love, clarity, focus, intuition, and confidence. This process allows us to know who we are, deepens our compassion and ability to love ourselves and others. This is the reason Rita is committed to providing the best natural products you will love to use and wear whether it's luxurious active-wear leggings to work out or meditate in, clean skincare, or creating a luxurious at home spa feeling with salt lamps, crystal book-ends, aromatherapy diffusers, natural essential oils, natural candles, all natural facial masks, crystals and much more. HappyBeingWell.com offers the tools/products, free educational resources, and inspiration to use in your daily spiritual and wellness practices.

Connect with Rita at www.HappyBeingWell.com

CHAPTER 40

I READ THE BIBLE

by Romy Faith Ganser
Holistic Health Practitioner, Romy Faith Wellness
https://Linktr.ee/RomyFaith

I don't recall ever having been as upset as I was at that one moment. I was despondent, unable to move. I could not compel my mouth to form words as my son was led out of the house late that spring evening in 2019. It wasn't my house. I had no control over the outcome of the fight. It wasn't the first time or the last. I wanted to help him, but nothing I did was the right thing. Hugs and kisses couldn't fix this.

I felt like my hands were bound and I needed comfort, too. So I prayed. In doing so I was reminded of a friend from church who had read the Bible four times. While reading, she had prayed for each of her children, prayed for their health and well-being, for their future successes. I knew this was the answer I was looking for. I had done Bible studies in various books of the Bible. Never had I read the entire book with intent. I bought a Bible for my son and I started reading. In the beginning God…

Noah was building an ark in Genesis and I began to feel my wounded spirit being lifted. When my son called, we hadn't spoken in five weeks. He felt my prayers and asked me to not stop.

In Exodus, Moses was leading the Israelites out of Egypt while we planned to meet for lunch.

God was presenting rules for worship to the priests in Leviticus when I heard from my son again. The conversations were becoming less tense, like the old days. He was thinking of going back to college to finish his degree.

I was reading in the book of Numbers when he called to share that he was registered to major in Liberal Arts. The dean of that department figured it would take three more years as all his credits wouldn't transfer. He said that was okay, he would do what he had to.

God was asking the Israelites to rededicate themselves to Him in Deuteronomy when I got another call. My new college student was very excited to share that he contacted the head of the Communications Department. By changing his major to communications all his credits would transfer and he would be done in three semesters rather than three years!

While I was in Joshua, he came for the weekend and we had a really nice visit! I was reading the book of Ruth while making plans for a weekend trip to Cape Cod with my boy.

The fall of that year was approaching and I was awed by the transformation of my relationship with my son and the positive actions he was taking. I had faith that my dedication to my daily prayer and reading of the Bible was impacting him. But I wasn't considering the possibilities of changes in my own life until a sunny day in September.

I was headed to my yoga class, but was running late. I texted the friends I ride with to say I would drive the carpool. That way they couldn't leave without me.

I opened the garage door and as it was opening a flurry of white caught my eye. I looked to find a pure white dove, in the garage, behind my car. I did the worldly things like check for a tag or some indication that this was someone's pet, but my soul knew that God's hand was in this.

I said hello to the bird and it approached me like a pet. I asked the Lord what He was trying to tell me. The Holy Spirit firmly told me, "be careful… be very, very, careful."

That dove was following my every step and trying to herd me away from the car. Instead of going back in the house I reached into the car for the phone. I called my friends and told them to go along without me. I assured them I would catch up as soon as I took care of something here. This agitated the dove so much that it flew up and hit the back of the car. Then it went back to pecking the ground staying under or in back of my car. I sat down in a chair outside my garage in an effort to wrap my head around what was happening and what it meant. I took some pictures and FaceTimed with my Mom. I had to prove this bird really was there and it wasn't my imagination. Twenty minutes went by and the dove didn't move away from my car. It was too late to get to yoga class by then. As I was saying the words, "I guess I'm not going anywhere now," the dove flew away in a grand flutter of white, its wingspan the size of an angel.

I had plans that evening and I wondered if it was safe to go. So in my mind I asked if it was okay to go out now. The answer from the Holy Spirit was, "Yes, the danger has passed." There was nothing wrong with my car. There were no accidents on the highway I could have been involved in. My belief is that there could have been had I not had the faith to believe in the Holy Spirit and His messenger.

My son graduated from college as I read the Psalms. Our relationship has improved and he recently moved across the country to pursue his dreams. I'm still praying for him and reading the Bible one chapter at a time. I know there are many more blessings yet to come. Amen.

ROMY FAITH GANSER

Romy Faith Ganser, BS, is a Holistic Health Practitioner. She is a graduate of the Institute for Integrative Nutrition where she earned her certification as a Holistic Health Coach. Romy also holds certifications in Chair Yoga Instruction and Reiki I & II. With these credentials, Romy has gained experience in patient advocacy, one-on-one and group counseling, and health education presentations.

Her passion has long been to share her knowledge of the body's innate and robust ability to heal itself. By aiding clients to better understand their physical, mental, and spiritual needs, she works with them to find their individual, optimal health. After graduating from Johnson and Wales University with a BS in Hospitality Management, she went on to spend three decades in the service industry, starting in food and hotel services, and then moving on to conference, event and trade show planning. Her skills of interpersonal communication, attention to detail and marketing, along with her thorough understanding of healthy food preparation and overall health education background, form a perfect foundation for Romy's position as a Holistic Health Practitioner. Romy holds memberships in several professional organizations, including her local Chamber of Commerce, Foundation for Wellness Professionals, and the American Association of Drugless Practitioners.

Connect with Romy here https://Linktr.ee/RomyFaith

CHAPTER 41

MASTER LEADERSHIP IN PUSHING UP PEOPLE

by Sabrina Protic
Financial Coach, World Class Partners Associates
https://www.sabrinaprotic.com/

To lead or to be lead, that is the question. For years I was in middle management with very strong upper management levels above me. For a time, I also managed a small administrative staff without any formal management training. Did I feel fulfilled and successful reporting to upper-management? Did I help my staff reach their full peak performance and potential? Truthfully, I never understood the components of leadership and management and where I fit best. I found myself complacent and just riding out the clock until retirement; even though I felt deep inside that I was underutilized. I lacked passion and purpose.

Have you heard it said, "Sometimes you make a decision, or one will be made for you"? I found myself unexpectedly unemployed due to pandemic cutbacks. The moment of truth had arrived: seek employment and come under management or become a business owner and a leader. I took a personal inventory of myself and determined that my passion was people. I loved networking with people, building teams of connectivity, support and collaboration. I opted to become an independent licensed financial coach to help people live their lives with financial confidence.

Mentorship is very important in developing leadership skills. I enrolled in a 10-week course at Pivot Point School for Financial Coaches. Part of the school's program was to purchase the book: *Pushing Up People* by Art Williams. When I started reading this book, I could not put it down. The principles in the book were what I needed to help me feel good about myself as well as help others to move forward in any capacity. As a financial coach, I could build a solo business or build a base shop as a team. I was learning the value of team and how to lead and be lead. An effective leader must understand the human spirit and how to elevate the team.

Hiring is equivalent to selecting teammates. Do you want to pick the best player or the player who is going to play their best, a hard worker over someone who does work hard? I learned that building a big team is less valuable than building a small hard-working team. Initially, I brought over 30 teammates quickly overlooking the Art Williams principles of hard work. I was pouring in, but not paying attention to the characteristics and makeup of the team. Did they embrace the vision? Who was willing to work hard? Who was willing to show up early and be there late, even on weekends? Who was willing to pay the price? My team deflated just as quickly as it inflated.

Art Williams quoted Vince Lombardi, "The dictionary is the only place that success comes before work." Hard work is the price we must pay for success. Art Williams says, "You have to pay the price. Sacrifice is part of the price." I have learned to look for potential teammates who are willing to work hard and as a result I have a great growing team.

This book taught me that it's not what I say, it's what I do. Art Williams says, "Do it first." A good leader leads by example, not just by words. Leaders do not stop leading once the success rolls in. We must continue to stay connected with our teams, remotely and in person, where possible. Every Saturday, I participate in a training session for newly licensed financial coaches and those studying to get their license. It's an hour and half out of my week where I show up and set the example of making time for them. I could have the attitude that I have my license and simply direct these newbies to show up for school. I am in the trenches with them. When I stop, some of them will stop, too. By my actions, I am teaching them to become leaders.

How then do we maintain these principles of pushing up people? Have you ever been talked down to by a leader in public or private? If so, did those words energize you to do more and reach peak performance? Or did you feel lowly, weak, and unproductive? The Art Williams system encourages leaders to make the team feel good by utilizing praise and recognition. There are times where an individual or the team needs readjusting and coaching. This should be done in the spirit of teaching and not with the sting of shaming. We should never embarrass or callout a person in front of others. Instead, we can use the group to our favor by stating processes, rules, and strategies to be achieved by everyone. No one person is singled out. Inside the message of praise, we are setting the bar of expectation. This is how we push up people. Underperformers know who they are. This person or the team will have the greatest of respect for leadership and will want to make improvements.

Do not fear Failure. It's going to happen. That is how we become the best at what we do. I have made my share of mistakes in learning new processes and techniques as a financial coach. I have to resist the temptation of dwelling on these mistakes and punishing myself mentally. "All you can do is all you can do – but all you can do is enough," Art Williams stresses in the book. This means we must give it our all in business and in the workplace. It's not going to be peaches and cream all time. We will fail. We will miss the mark. However, we will know that we did everything within our power to make it happen. Move on. "Success is never certain, and failure is never final." I have saved this quote from Art Williams to refer to when I hit the lows. I must tell you that Leadership is where I can do the most good for the most people. I grow each time I help someone else grow. I found my calling, my purpose, and my passion. Referring to The Art Williams system continues to help me keep myself in balance.

SABRINA PROTIC

Sabrina Protic is an energetic and vibrant wife, mother, and grand-mother. She loves educating and empowering her community as a Licensed World-Class Financial Coach, Certified Life Coach, Author of the Book *Growing Ageless, Think Young-Live Younger*, collaborative author of *Top 25 Change Makers, Keep Smiling Dose of Hope, Wellness for Winners*, and International Streaming Live Co-Host of Thriving Women Talk.

Sabrina is the founder of W.E.E. Women's Entrepreneurial Empowerment, an organization striving for continuous opportunities for women to expand their networks, develop relationships, and grow their businesses. Sabrina is the co-founder of The Sharper Woman Newsletter, a resource to help women live longer, younger, stronger, and smarter lives utilizing the power of information. Sabrina is also the COO of Thriving Women Network airing on E360TV.

Learn more about Sabrina at www.SabrinaProtic.com

CHAPTER 42

IGNITE TO WIN

by Sandra Barker-McIntosh
Founder, 90 Day Wins LLC
www.90daywins.com

This book found me at the right time in my life. Before reading *Think and Grow Rich*, I went along with the flow. I was existing and being frustrated with life. I did not have a clear purpose. I was doing what others expected of me. I wanted to please everyone but myself. And follow the path I was supposed to follow. I was trying to live up to other people's standards. Doing this made me frustrated and confused. I was ready for a change.

I was studying for my CPA license. Each day I would spend at least three hours studying for the Test. I kept wondering if this was what I was supposed to be looking forward to in my career. Deep down, I did not want to be a CPA. I was over accounting. I did not enjoy it anymore. I had no desire to be in a monthly meeting discussing financial statements. I no longer cared about the work I had spent over 20 years doing. I desired a new path. But I had no idea how to make the changes I desperately wanted. I was unhappy at work and home. I would complain to my family about the time to devote to studying. I was sick of the endless questions from friends and co-workers about how I was studying and when I would retake the exam. The CPA exam consumed my life. Until I read *Think and Grow Rich*.

One evening after complaining to a friend, she encouraged me to join a Mastermind group for women entrepreneurs. She mentioned the group would read *Think and Grow Rich* and discuss each chapter weekly. I remember her asking me if I had ever read the book. Nope, that was my reply.

I've heard of it but never read it. I never really desired to read a book telling me to grow rich. But I was intrigued to try something new with these ladies.

We read a chapter of *Think and Grow Rich* by Napoleon Hill each week.

I heard many positive stories of people learning and growing from reading this book. I knew I was ready for change.

And so, my journey began. I went to a nearby second-hand bookstore and bought my first copy.

Reading it lit a spark inside of me. I was intrigued by what I would find helpful in my life from this book. I was tired of the status quo. All I knew was I was ready to make changes.

"Desire – the first step towards riches." It seemed as if my life would change drastically from the first chapter. I now understand I was committed and ready for this change. I became convicted by reading this first chapter. I had decided to no longer waste any more of my precious time studying for the CPA exam. I desired more. I had allowed other people to tell me what I should be. This chapter encouraged me to Believe in Sandra. Do what I genuinely want to do. And not care what anyone else thought of my decisions. I realized I was not living my life to the fullest. Many would think to judge and ask me why. But I was not afraid anymore. I read, "we win, or we perish." And I knew I was ready to Win.

Something about reading "**we win or we perish**." I did not know how or what this meant for my life. But I was determined to find out.

It made me feel very confident and created a deep passion for learning from Napoleon Hill's adventures in making this book.

Each week I began asking myself powerful questions after reviewing each with the mastermind group. I would no longer continue to live a lie. I had to be honest with myself.

I was good at Accounting. Managing multiple teams helped each company I worked with achieve its goals. But I was unfulfilled. I desired more for my life. I wanted to achieve goals in my personal life.

Reading *Think and Grow Rich* inspired me to dream bigger. To believe I was worthy of the dreams I wanted.

In the same way, I achieved goals quarterly in my corporate accounting work. I needed to ignite my fire. I desired a result that would allow me to make an impact. As I read about faith and persistence, I became more excited about my future. Who would help me achieve my goals? I started to put together the vision for my life. I talked with friends and family, telling them about my adventure. After reading *Think and Grow Rich*, I decided to create my 90 Day Wins process. The 90 Day Wins process allowed me to create a quarterly plan for achieving goals. I introduced this process to my employees and family. Everyone has a goal or two they desire to accomplish. I found joy in working towards my goals quarterly with my team. And they were achieving goals and excited to celebrate wins. We started completing projects before deadlines. I became motivated to dream bigger. To pursue my personal goals. I found the courage to start my 90 Day Wins podcast. Because I had this newfound courage to pursue my dreams, I was no longer afraid to learn new things. I am now willing to ask for assistance from experts. This book allowed me to ignite my fire within. To step out on faith and achieve my goals.

As I have learned, many people just don't get it. They don't get the excitement that this book created for me. They don't get how a book written so many years ago could inspire me to make such radical changes in my life.

The beautiful thing about it is that I don't care what other people think or say. I am igniting my passion. I am willing to bet on myself every day. I can grow and learn and fail and get back up and win.

SANDRA BARKER-MCINTOSH

Sandra Barker-McIntosh is an accountant turned coach, author, and podcast creator with over 20 years of experience in corporate America. Over the years, Sandra has leveraged her professional experience and optimism to offer accountability, life, and career coaching services.

She is particularly passionate about catering her coaching to women ready for wins in their personal and professional lives.

Sandra is the host and creator of the podcast 90 Day Wins, where she discusses topics related to goal-achieving and life lessons. 90 Day Wins is an inspiring process that guides her coaching and professional achievements; it allows her and the individuals and groups she coaches to achieve their goals every 90 days.

Sandra is a determined goal-getter and natural-born leader who is inspired and encouraged by the people she interviews on her podcast and is inspired by their intention and drive to reach their goals.

Sandra is a devoted wife and mom. When she is not working, she enjoys spending time with her family traveling, planning new adventures, competing in 5K mud runs, and exploring nature. She believes the motto, "Work hard, Play Harder," is a cornerstone to success.

Sandra is a certified Personal & Executive Coach, Author, and Podcaster and holds an MBA in Accounting.

Connect with Sandra here: www.90daywins.com

CHAPTER 43

DISCOVERING ME

by Shanna Lee Moore
Owner, Developing True Health and Justice Massage
www.developingtruehealth.com

Discovering me on a journey of growing,
Searching inside until I find the knowing.

When we are first born, we're perfect and whole,
Sometimes when there's trauma it creates a big hole.

These agreements I've made to remind me you see,
Of all the power I have to be authentically me.

The me who has confidence and acts with love,
The me who was created by Him up above.

I use my words to speak truth and light,
They illuminate the path because they are so bright.

I don't allow others to decide my fate,
This is my life and it is going to be great!

We know what they say about the word assume,
Not having clarity can lead to doom.

The best I have is the best you'll get,
That's how I can avoid living with regret.

The Four Agreements have changed my life,
They've brought me peace and taken away strife.

The wisdom I value like that of fine pearls,
So much so that I've shared it with my girls.

Now they can continue to pass on the insights,
Freedom is one of our basic rights.

Freedom begins inside our own mind,
Examine yours to see what you find.

If you're limited in your beliefs or expression,
Perhaps this book will provide a new lesson.

20 years ago I was in a season of transition. Growing into an adult, leaving childhood and old survival skills behind. Learning about myself and who I wanted to show up as in the world. I have held one book dear to my heart and have given it credit for the foundation of who I have become over the years. Whenever I've been asked what my favorite book is, this is the first to come to mind. I believe that we could change the world by learning and applying the principles in Don Miguel Ruiz's *The Four Agreements* as a collective. I have read this book four times so far. The principles are simple, yet powerful. Each agreement, when implemented, can create positive changes in your life. It did in mine.

Writing those words, "as a collective," is very powerful because I have actually found a community who has done just that. It is refreshing and invigorating to have these four simple agreements in the forefront of my mind when traveling on the journey of life. Also, by surrounding myself with others who have chosen to live this way, I've created a heightened experience. I finally found my tribe. We can witness our growth and be a reflection to each other in the group. We cheer on each other and hold space when needed. We share our dreams and goals, then celebrate their manifestation into reality.

Each time I read through this book I get reminded of the power that lies within me and every being on Earth. We are in the midst of an awakening. We are becoming more conscious each day. We are learning about the ability we have to change ourselves and, in turn, change our world. I no longer need to be a slave or victim to my circumstances. I no longer need to share pain to relate to others. I have pulled away layers of myself like an onion and embraced my authentic self. It has taken me many years to get here. We are all works in progress. These agreements I make first to myself and second to those I come into contact with. My path to self-discovery and personal freedom will be an ongoing one. I will strive to grow on a daily basis and implement all that I have learned.

My favorite experience reading through this book was the round with my youngest daughter. She was 10 years old at the time of her first exposure. I take great joy in knowing that she now has 10 years longer than I did to utilize these principles in her life. One of my dreams is to teach my children tools to equip them to have their best lives possible. It is the same dream I have for my community. To be a resource and inspire action. To ask questions like "What Else is Possible?" To feel in alignment with my passion and purpose and share my gifts with the world.

How have I changed from reading this book and applying the principles? I learned that I have the power within myself and my thinking to not let anything or anyone steal my joy. That I can show up powerfully in my authenticity and uniqueness as my true self. That I can love myself regardless of outside circumstances. And that my best is good enough.

I used to be negative and complain quite often. I now better understand the power behind my words. I pause with a breath and ponder whether or not what I want to say is productive or destructive. I don't take criticism to heart. I love myself and am aware that not everyone is as far along on their journey as I am. This of course is a little more challenging with those closer relationships, such as immediate family, than it is with strangers. Even when I'm feeling down about something someone said or did, I don't let it affect me too long. A boat cannot sink unless water gets inside it. I have learned to communicate more directly instead of in a passive aggressive way. I have started to ask clarifying questions and listen for the answers. When I feel that I missed something, I can admit my shortcomings and learn from the experience without too much judgment. The last one allows me the grace I need to continue on my path.

As long as I follow these agreements I know I can live my best life.

Thank you for reading. I look forward to connecting soon.

SHANNA LEE MOORE

Shanna Lee Moore is an entrepreneur, business owner, and Award-Winning, International #1 Bestselling Author. Shanna has been a licensed massage therapist in San Diego, California, since 2007.

Shanna began sharing the benefits of electrolyzed, reduced water in 2012 after being introduced to it and having a personal life changing experience.

Since 2020, Shanna has focused more on building her community, growing more with personal and professional development, sharing her stories and poems in books and speaking at virtual events to inspire others.

Her passion is helping others create the life they've always wanted. Shanna offers creative solutions and out-of-the-box thinking to help people balance their families and businesses.

Shanna loves connecting with motivated, passionate people both in person and virtually.

Connect with Shanna :

https://calendly.com/shannaleemoore/30min

CHAPTER 44

YOUR STORY: IT'S A JOURNEY

by Sherri Leopold
CEO of Dream BIG with Sherri Leopold
https://sherrileopold.com

Most of the reading I have done over the past 25 years has been in either personal development or business. One of the most impactful books I have read is called *Building a Story Brand: Clarify Your Message So Your Customers Will Listen* by Donald Miller. He describes seven elements of great storytelling to grow your business. This was absolutely impactful in my business, but impactful in my personal life as well. As I learned the formula and started to apply the knowledge, the quality of my customers changed as well as my ability to guide them. Our story, or our message, is so important and deserves to be told. Telling it well makes a big difference in success.

You might wonder how? Our life is a story. We create it, write the scenes, tell and live the story, and close deals through our entire lifetime. Deals?! Yes, deals. We engage in relationships, friendships, enroll in college, buy homes, get married, go through divorces, have children, and so many more deals. Each story we write in our lives mirrors a certain framework. It's the same formula that is used in story branding in movies, and in YOUR story and in mine. He calls it the Story Brand Formula or the SB 7 Framework.

To quote Donald Miller from page 20, "Here is every story you see or hear in a nutshell: A CHARACTER who wants something, encounters a PROBLEM before they can get it. At the peak of their despair, a GUIDE steps into their lives, gives them a PLAN, and CALLS THEM TO ACTION. That action helps them avoid FAILURE and ends in a SUCCESS."

In December of 2013, I considered joining a new MLM. I had been in my current company for less than 6 months. If I moved and pursued this opportunity, this would be my 10th different company in 16 years. The first problem: Would people trust me, or even do business with me anymore? I didn't know.

Problem two, the company had only been in business for 15 months. No one knew what it was. I had never encountered this before. I had no experience in sharing something so new that no one had any familiarity or trust in it. In the story brand of MY life, I was that customer with the problem. Enter a series of guides that would help. Many times, there was simply one guide; in this case there were quite a few. These guides were Carol Miller, Britney Beneke, Sheila Fausone, Mauria Dillard, and Toni Strathman. I wanted success in a way that I had never had, and they helped create the plan to get there. This was delivered through corporate conference calls, training guides, encouragement, and coaching calls. This helped me avoid failure and achieve success, which is exactly what the formula teaches. WOW! I had no idea all of this was creating MY story.

Each of these guides had their own type of call to action, yet the same intent to help me succeed! (Calls to action are always either to help you succeed or to avoid failure.) In this case, the call to action and the plan from the guides was to hit the 12K rank (monthly sales) and earn my very first auto bonus. I had fallen short in every other prior company. This goal had eluded me until now.

I followed the steps of the plan and succeeded in hitting that 12K auto bonus goal four months after I started! Like a typical great movie, I succeeded. I overcame my problem with the help of my guides and avoided failure and succeeded in being the hero in my own story! My story has helped me guide others through their story.

One of the most fabulous aspects of this book is that Donald Miller uses very well-known movies to explain in detail, enabling us to understand the story brand and the formula. It's fascinating to realize that the formula is mirrored in life as well and gives new meaning to the cliché of art imitating life.

I learned how to share my story so that people are interested in it. More importantly, this book helped me understand my customer's journey. I am a customer too, but I rarely stop to think about "how" I am making my decisions. I am now much more sensitive to how I am writing sales copy, my language in emails, and how I respond to my customers. This has completely transformed how I interact with my customers after being in business for 24 years. I am better at client relationships as a result.

One of the most important aspects of this book is that he teaches you to see things through your customers' eyes. He positions you as the customer in your own business. It reminds me of something I learned from Speaker Joel Weldon. Always use TLC; but not tender loving care. His TLC means Think Like a Customer. This is something I use every single day. I never send a message before first asking myself what I would think if it were sent to me. I have become acutely aware of my customers' journey and how I interact with them. I am honored to be part of their story. I am so grateful to be the person who is able to share and guide my customers. Understanding what my customer needs at such a fundamental level has changed how I do business. I am aware of my customers' needs today from what I learned in this book.

It's changed how I view my customers. It's changed how I serve my customers. Most of all, it has transformed me. It has affirmed how important our stories are.

Your story matters.

How you tell it matters.

You deserve to be understood.

I see you, I hear you, and I understand you. I will guide you as the hero in YOUR story if I am ever blessed to do so.

SHERRI LEOPOLD

Sherri Leopold is the Leader of the Stop Self- Bullying Movement, Mentor, Author, Speaker, CEO of Dream Big with Sherri Leopold. Sherri has authored 8 books including 6 International Best-Selling books. She loves working and collaborating with others. She's worked in the Network Marketing/Direct Selling industry for 24 years, sharing her expertise in speaking, mentoring, and team building. She has earned 25 incentive trips in those 24 years. Twenty of those trips have been earned in the past 8 years with her current company, Le-Vel, a leader in the health and wellness industry. She is a 200K Leader and has developed a thriving community of leaders. Sherri also hosts the television show Outside the Box with Sherri Leopold on Legrity Media TV. She loves shining a light on other servant leaders who are making a difference in the world. She resides in Springfield IL, USA where she is passionate about encouraging others to live the life they deserve and create financial freedom.

Connect with Sherri at www.SherriLeopold.com

CHAPTER 45

CHEESE OPENED MY EYES

by JoEllen "aka Sohaila" Handelsman
Owner, SohailaInternational LLC
www.SohailaInternational.com

Life is rich in changes. Without change we can't grow. I have had this book *Who Moved My Cheese?* by Spencer Johnson sitting on my bookshelf for years. It's nestled around other motivational and uplifting books that I have been meaning to read. One day I was walking past my bookshelf in my office and I turned and glanced at all my books. *Who Moved My Cheese?* caught my eye. I took it off the shelf and dusted the bits of dust off it and began reading.

Going back 40 years, my life has been filled with changes, good and bad, though without the bad, you can't appreciate the good.

You see, I became a professional belly dance artist at the age of 17. I never thought in my wildest dreams that I was going to be a professional dance artist and travel the world. In fact, I wanted to be a cop, yes, a police officer 'to protect and serve' ever since I was in the 8th grade. Well, long story short, I became a professional dancer, dancing in many countries around the world.

Now, I know what you are wondering, how did this book change my life? *Cheese* resonated with me because when I started traveling I wanted to do everything I could do now... now... now. And I did. My motto has always been, "Why wait, do it now." I am glad I had that mentality as I traveled and danced around the world. With this mentality, I saw so many places. By the time I was 24 I saw half of the world and had done things that most people only dream of. It wasn't until I came back from dancing in the Middle East in 1997 that I became aware that more changes lay ahead.

I started teaching more, becoming a professor in dance, and received my Bachelor's Degree. With my professional imminence, it reflected as a Master's Degree in dance.

As I kept reading *Cheese*, I saw my life pass before my eyes, seeing the different chapters of my life by running here and running there. Even though I still live with my "why wait" approach, I find that the older I get the 'wiser' I become. I know this is part of life, a big part.

I've learned that life is a great experience and there will be changes every day. This book helped me to understand how to better handle the changes in my life and how to avoid the pitfalls as they arrive. I have learned to anticipate and prepare for change, overcome fears, envision more success, and enjoy change to the fullest. After all, "Life is too short, do everything you want and can now" is what I have adapted over the years. I believe that what you set out to do you can seek the success you deserve. And always remember, don't ever give up on your dreams!

I used to make things a bit complicated. Even though I still tend to do this in some situations, I stop and go back to *Cheese* and that is when I take a deep breath, slow down, and think about the situation. I have learned to listen more to my own intuition instead of diving head first.

I've also learned to not take things in my life for granted. I used to assume that things would always be there when I wanted or needed… until it wasn't.

If we don't pay attention, one day that "cheese" will be gone and it will force you to open your eyes. *Cheese* helped me to learn and cope with changes. After all, if you want to thrive and survive, you will need to make changes. It's what you do with those changes that will make a difference in your life. This is what makes life complete, for now anyway, until the next change is needed.

Change and take action.

Needless to say, I have been searching and craving for my stock of cheese for over 40 years. Even though I have been very successful, deep down I am still looking for that bliss. Does it ever get better than this? I am very happy. Maybe it doesn't get better than this, but if it does, I will be there looking for it and waiting for it. I say to you, "Embrace whatever change comes to you!"

Change happens whether we like it or not and change is inevitable no matter where you are in life. I now check in daily with changes that are taking place and don't take this time for granted. I strive to think outside the box and find new ways to approach changes.

How did this book transform my life, you ask…. It is still transforming my life by thinking and listening to my gut feeling and moving forward.

SOHAILA HANDELSMAN

Jo Ellen aka "Sohaila" Handelsman has traveled the world as a dance entrepreneur expert for over 40+ years. Her travels have led to meeting dynamic people from around the globe. Her infectious enthusiasm for everything she sets out to do is priority in her life, and this is why she is so successful.

Sohaila is a Motivational Speaker, Best-Selling Author, Digital Marketer and Professor of Middle Eastern Dance with a Bachelor's Degree in Dance. She is the founder of Sohaila International, an umbrella for The Sense-ual Woman® program and retreats, Belly dance and NewVo® dance fitness classes in her studio and via Zoom™. She is the author of five books on Middle Eastern dance and holistic healing, and has created numerous signature dance DVDs, and hosts her own Sohaila TV for empowering entrepreneurs to be the C.E.O of their own life. With 45 years traveling around the world, dancing has led her to interact with different cultures and clients. Sohaila helps women Entrepreneurs to stop feeling invisible and start becoming INVINCIBLE by integrating movement and mindset in a whole new way. Women rediscover something more powerful within themselves, experiencing more joy, more confidence and blessings in their life, not to mention attracting a flood of their ideal clients! Sohaila also is a Real Estate specialist catering to high end clientele. Sohaila is just a phone call away with your entrepreneurial or real estate needs.

Contact Sohaila here: www.SohailaInternational.com

CHAPTER 46

QUESTIONING WHAT YOU BELIEVE TO BE TRUE

by Teresa Cundiff
CEO of Wordy Nerds Media, Inc.
https://teresatalkstv.com

We look in the mirror at ourselves every day. Usually in a utilitarian way as we need to brush our teeth and fix our hair, plus a lot of us females like to apply makeup. I'll admit that for me it's vanity because I feel the best about myself when my hair and makeup are done. However, I don't spend countless hours in front of the mirror. Who has time for that? I must be efficient with the minutes that I have allotted myself for the morning rituals, but I will be honest here. On the mornings when I'm out the door at 0430, the makeup time doesn't happen.

Then there's the metaphorical mirror. I used to read books strictly for entertainment. It hasn't been until the last year that I have read books for self-development. And it wasn't until I began my interview-style Teresa Talks TV show that I started reading books that may not have come into my sphere at all. I am very opinionated about the authors I read and interviewing the authors of those books has been a treat for me. For example, I won't read an author that Oprah picks. I tried for a year when we lived in the Chicago area. I even went to two of her book club shows, but I discovered that I hated every one of her authors' books! I will give a book 100 pages before I slam it shut and put it down which is more than some books deserve.

When I read *My Life with Karma* by Travis Sackett, I was blown away by so many things I learned about myself. Or let me rephrase…

so many things I thought I knew to be true about myself but weren't. Let me explain.

I have lived a blessed life in so many ways. I have been touched by some tragedy and trauma that has changed me forever, but I never had anyone I loved become addicted to drugs of any sort. However, I had a beloved cousin who was bipolar and at the young age of 28 died tragically in a car accident by driving recklessly. So, my life has been touched by mental illness. My daddy was an alcoholic when I was little, but he put the stuff down when he gave his life to Christ, and we never even had alcohol in the house after that.

I always thought people with addictions lacked self-control and were selfish. That "those people" could just stop if they wanted to and that they just didn't want to. At least, I think that's what I thought? I mean, I'm not completely sure I had a position. It had just never been part of my life to really have to take up a position. I only knew what was said on the news about the opioid crisis and had no proper understanding of the drug world at all. I take my prescriptions from my doctor for my Rheumatoid Arthritis, and I am grateful for them because I would surely be a cripple without them and live a life wracked with pain. I surely know the pain of barely being able to walk without the aid of pharmaceuticals.

We've all seen how drug addicts are portrayed in movies. They are in filthy houses with dirt-stained sofas and mattresses strewn everywhere with needles hanging out of their arms all strung out. With no frame of reference to the contrary, I allowed this image to exist as the way it must be. Of course the opioid crisis stood all these stereotypes on their heads when now the drugs creating the addicts were prescribed by doctors.

I ordered *My Life with Karma* because I was intrigued by the "cop turned criminal" angle. I needed to check this out for myself. Once I read it, I couldn't get on the phone with the author fast enough. I had to talk to the incredible young man who had lived such an enthralling story. The fact that he was still alive to tell his story was nothing short of a miracle, and I just had to know him. He didn't know me from anyone, but I felt like I needed some redemption because of these prejudices that I had but yet, at the same time, I didn't realize that I had, truly. Had I looked down my nose at the addict and not wanted to offer help? Is that what Jesus would do? How many other addicts' stories were just like Travis'? How many people react just like me to the words, "He's an addict"?

This book is turning some of what I believed to be true about many institutions inside out! This book has changed me, and that's why *My Life with Karma* is *The Book I Read* that has profoundly impacted me. I want to have more discernment in my life. I don't want to judge "books" by their covers for bad or for GOOD! I know that I am fundamentally flawed because I see things in black and white and nothing really is. Travis Sackett's book has brought me to an awareness that I did not have before reading it. A place where people do make poor decisions, but then, people also place their trust in professionals and institutions and get abused. Not all, but some.

We want to trust that our doctors are caring for us properly. We want to trust that our law enforcement is caring for us properly. My problem is having a strong sense of right and wrong. I can't process why people want to intentionally inflict pain on others. I come away from reading this book a changed woman with my heart slightly broken. The book has stuck with me since the day I read it.

I realize that I must not label people as I do not want to be labelled. I see the people begging at the intersections and know that more compassion is required and less cynicism. People are hurt and have been hurt and more is required of me, and I must be willing to give it.

TERESA CUNDIFF

Teresa Cundiff is CEO of Wordy Nerds Media, Inc. which produces her digital streaming TV show Teresa Talks, of which Legrity.TV is the Executive Producer. The show tagline is "Inspiring Conversations with Authors: Published & Unpublished!" An unpublished author just means those authors who haven't put their books on paper yet. The show provides a platform for authors to have a global reach with their message. It can be seen on Roku, AppleTV, GoogleTV, Amazon Fire, and Smart TVs.

Teresa is also a Freelance Proofreader with the tagline, "I know where the commas go!" Teresa makes her clients' work shine with her knowledge of grammar, punctuation, and sentence structure.

Teresa is a Four-Time International Best-Selling contributing author of 1 Habit for Entrepreneurial Success, 1 Habit to Thrive in a Post-COVID World, The Art of Connection: 365 Days of Networking Quotes & The Art of Connection: 365 Days of Inspirational Quotes with the latter two being placed in the Library of Congress.

Teresa is also a Four-Time Best-Selling author as one of 33 authors in *The 13 Steps to Riches* Series published through Habitude Warriors where each book is based on one of the 13 Principles of *Think & Grow Rich* by Napoleon Hill.

Teresa and her husband Brian live in Fredericksburg, Virginia, have two sons, one daughter-in-love, and a grandson due in April!

Connect with Teresa at https://teresatalkstv.com

CHAPTER 47

VISIONARIES DISREGARD PARADIGMS AND REINVENT

by Terry Shepherd
Founder, Ramirez & Clark Publishers
www.ramirezandclark.com

When I was a senior in high school, I became fascinated with the common denominators all successful people shared. What magic blueprint created uncommon achievement? Earl Nightingale's cassette, "20 Minutes That Can Change Your Life," taught me how The Goldmine between your ears is the catalyst to create innovative new approaches to fulfill enduring needs. I discovered The Formula 'Our rewards in life will always be in direct proportion to our service,' and The Word 'Attitude.'

A lesson learned growing up during seismic shifts in culture, the Vietnam war, the women's movement, and the press for Civil Rights, was how every situation presented an opportunity. Our job was to figure out what it was.

So, it was natural that I would discover Dale Carnegie.

Dale died the year I was born. Yet his treasure, *How to Win Friends and Influence People*, was still a best-seller, nineteen years after its first printing in 1936. Dismissed by many scholars as a layman's how-to book, it didn't get much academic attention. But it continues to resonate with readers today, thirty million copies later. It's the foundation for Keith Ferrazzi's twenty-first century relationship classic, *Never Eat Alone*, has connections to Jim Collins' *Good to Great*. And it helped spawn the self-help industry, modern motivational speaking, and influenced the lives and careers of a wide variety of notable people from comedian Lenny Bruce to billionaire Warren Buffett.

Reading Carnegie was the beginning of my own career trajectory, leading to the corporate executive suite, entrepreneurship, and the clarity of life purpose, still central to who I am today.

Such was the fire in my heart for the book, that I decided to memorize it.

I created a poem to distill the essence of each chapter into simple words which would trigger my mind to recall and act on the key ideas. Here's an example:

Appreciate, don't criticize, and meet their needs

Sincere interest plants the seeds

Remember names and always smile

Get them to talk and listen while

About their interests you converse

And make them feel important first

In college, I discovered how Carnegie's philosophies are based on age-old psychological concepts which can motivate someone to want to help you achieve your goals. One of the most dominant is a version of Earl Nightingale's formula: Others evaluate their relationship with us in direct proportion to the value we add to their lives.

This idea is the underpinning of all business relationships. We buy from people we like and trust; people who make us feel valued and are genuinely interested in our own needs. The more value we add, the more we can earn.

The notion of sincerity, authenticity, appreciation, and the importance of serving others has biblical connections, is linked to successful marriages, stellar careers, effective parenting, and political power.

On the dark side, *How to Win Friends and Influence People*, was one of the tools utilized by the leaders of Nazi Germany to seduce the populace. Charles Manson is said to have used the ideas in the book to convince women to kill people on his orders.

But the work's overwhelming impact has been connected to compassionate caring. It overlays the life and work of icons like Mahatma Gandhi and Mother Teresa. Dozens of modern leadership books reference Carnegie as a resource. Maya Angelou may well have been thinking of Carnegie when she penned her iconic quote, "I've learned that people will forget what you said, people will forget what you did, but people will never forget how you made them feel."

In my own interviews with successful men and women, I've often seen dog-eared copies of *How to Win Friends and Influence People*, close at hand and certificates of Dale Carnegie Course completion hanging next to college degrees on office walls.

So, what is the ultimate essence of this book?

Getting what you want requires helping others get what they want. This is a classic paraphrase of a Zig Ziglar motivational chestnut. Keith Ferrazzi adds an important postscript. To earn an exponential return on your investment of time, talent, and treasure, you must give *without the expectation of return.*

Faith that your acts of kindness will reflect back on you is essential, because many of our investments in things like education, relationships, and ideas take time to mature. The IF / THEN binary defining The Law of Cause and Effect is not instantaneous. But it is inevitable.

We are motivated by patterns of behavior, not single instances. A body of work takes time to build.

Nearly five decades after first reading this simple, yet powerful, book, I find myself returning to it to refresh my spirit and recharge the behaviors so central to my ability to add value, provide for my family, and create a series of career inventions which enriched my soul even more deeply than they have filled my bank account.

Life is a roller coaster ride. We can't have the ups without the downs. Plot twists constantly appear. We must adapt and overcome. Failure is essential to growth. A key metric is not how often we fail, but how often we can get back up. Purpose drives passion. Passion leads to excellence. And monetary rewards are almost always the result of excellent execution of a thoughtful plan based on a meaningful mission.

As our family has dealt with changing job markets, health adventures, the beginning of new lives, and the inevitable goodbyes that are part of every journey, the words in *How to Win Friends and Influence People*, still whisper their wisdom. They are evident everywhere.

The first question we ask each morning is: How can I make one life better today. The last? How well did I do it?

Our ability to deploy our Goldmine, The Formula and The Word in every situation can lead from one achievement to the next, creating a body of work which will ripple across the ages, long after our own names are forgotten.

And that is life's ultimate purpose.

TERRY SHEPHERD

Terry Shepherd created Detective Jessica Ramirez in 2019, publishing his thriller *Chasing Vega* in 2020. The book earned 5-Star ratings on Amazon and is also available in audiobook and Spanish language editions. *Chasing the Captain* was released to stellar reviews in 2021. *Chasing Karma*, the third book in the Jessica Ramirez trilogy is due out in 2022. He created the *Waterford Detective* stories for his grandson and published the popular *Juliette and the Mystery Bug* series, co-authored with his wife, Colleen, when his granddaughter wondered how kids could protect themselves during a pandemic. He wrote *Students In Time*, a time travel adventure that parallels the 4th grade public school history curriculum.

Terry is also a prolific audio-artist, narrating 7 novels, along with dozens of commercials and promotional trailers. He hosts the popular Authors on the Air podcast, and was an early social media adopter, authoring *Social Media and Your Personal Brand* in 2012.

He has written over 400 motivational essays since 2004, the best of which were aggregated into three popular self-help books.

Terry and Colleen live on the ocean in Jacksonville, Florida and are co-founders of "Down Syndrome Nation," a web resource for friends and families of persons with Down syndrome. Terry studied at Michigan State University, Harvard and Oxford and toured South America as a rock drummer in the summer of 1972.

Connect with Terry here: www.ramirezandclark.com

CHAPTER 48

A TASTE OF HEALING

by Tweet Larkin

Inspiration can come from different avenues and at times when you least expect it. When inspiration hits you, it will motivate you in ways you never imagined. It will make you feel like you are empowered to make life changes that are desperately needed.

I've lived with a chronic condition my entire life. Ever since I could remember, the number of days where I felt normal or healthy have been very minimal. Starting out at a young age, nausea, vomiting and diarrhea have always been part of my daily routine. The constant feeling of exhaustion only offset by the fear of my next "episode" was overwhelming.

My course changed in the summer of 2009. In fact, it wasn't until I was recently asked what book inspired you that I realized the impact of this change. My first thought kind of shocked me, but many say always go with your gut instinct because that is the most reliable guide and should be trusted. It's the most unconventional book, but it had the most impact on me when I needed it the most. Believe it or not, the book that changed my course and inspired me the most was a cookbook. Not a normal cookbook; however, it was a cookbook for gluten free recipes.

I was in 4th grade the first time my mother took me to visit the doctor to address my condition. It was during that time that my episodes became much more frequent. What used to occur once every month or so grew into 1 to 2 times per week… for months on end.

Unfortunately, at the time, no pattern was present thus making it very difficult for the doctor to establish any real answers. The doctor suggested I not eat anything with lactose and to avoid fruits and vegetables. However, going on this "diet" didn't improve my situation. My episodes still occurred and I just learned to live with it.

Many years went by and I soon found myself married with two kids. But my symptoms continued. Not only did I feel lost, but it was now interfering with the lives of my family. With my symptoms getting out of control, I found myself heading back to another doctor for answers. This one was the most difficult. She told me it was all in my head and that I needed to see a counselor. She quickly prescribed me an anti-depressant basically telling me I was crazy. The sad part is when you have constant vomiting, diarrhea, nausea it will cause you to not want to eat which then will bring about anxieties which can get so out of control you have a feeling of being lost. I was beginning to feel this doctor was right.

So, I took the doctor's advice and visited with a counselor, and what a great decision that was. He started by telling me exactly what I needed to hear, "It's not in your head!" He went on to provide me with the name and number of a very good GI doctor. I'm not a crier, but when those words hit my ears and hearing his reassurance, I couldn't contain the tears. As I sat there and ugly cried in his office, I realized I was so very lost. Once leaving his office I made the call to the doctor and at my first visit with him I ugly cried once more. This doctor knew exactly what had been plaguing me since as far back as I could remember. He ordered a test that forever changed my life.

The test revealed I had gastroparesis, which means your stomach periodically suffers from paralysis. It becomes unable to digest food so you either vomit to rid yourself of its contents or it gets so overprocessed in your stomach that it's passed into your intestines. Your intestines then sound the alarm tell your body to get rid of the poison. That's when you go into full on violent vomiting with intestinal discomfort and it doesn't care when or where you are. No matter how many times it happens, you never get used to it and it always feels like you're going to die.

Sadly, even with the diagnosis, life still did not improve. Unfortunately, it's a chronic condition with very little options in the way of meds to help manage it. My symptoms persisted and now were causing my anxieties to control and rule my life. At this point, defeat was in front of me. Death could have been right around the corner for me and I could care less.

Then something changed. A life event occurred. I read about gluten intolerance and the impact it can have on people, especially those with chronic intestinal conditions. Within minutes, I found myself at the local bookstore. On the shelf I found a cookbook, *Gluten Free Recipes*. This simple purchase changed my course.

For the first time in my life, this little cookbook started my journey. I stopped looking to others for answers but, instead, began to look within. It allowed me to stop hating myself and instead start to heal. Going gluten free and having that gluten free recipe book helped to guide me and provide ideas that helped with my stomach issues. Through that book, my life was back on the right path to living again. The book inspired me to take control over my life by the choices of food I was putting in my body allowing me to heal and have less episodes from my chronic illness. And the crazy thing is, I didn't realize the importance of this book until I was asked the question, "What book transformed your life?" Going gluten free and having that gluten free recipe book to help guide me gave me ideas that helped with my stomach issues. Through that book, I started living again.

The Best Gluten-Free cookbook by Donna Washburn and Heather Butt might not have been intended for gastroparesis, but it certainly helped me gain my life back. Meals that were comfort meals were still allowed and recipes showed me I wasn't limited as much as the disease made me feel. My favorite by far was the blueberry muffin recipe. By removing gluten from my food, it became easier for my stomach to digest which made my episodes become less frequent. Having a break from gastroparesis is such a relief.

TWEET LARKIN

Tweet Larkin has been married for 26 years to her high school sweetheart with two kids living every day the way most do. Growing up in Connecticut in a small town, she played many different sports to pass time as a child. Once her children were grown, she went back to school to become a medical assistant where she graduated with honors. Up until recently, she worked as a medical assistant working for a primary care physician for an amazing doctor and co-workers. She truly enjoyed her job and made long friendships with many of the patients.

Her life is about to change since she and her family are making a move south. Currently living in New England where it's truly beautiful and the changes of the seasons will be missed but looking forward to being outside all year long is something Tweet has been looking forward to for a long time. The best part of the day is when the sun is bright, and you can feel the warmth from it, being able to enjoy the simple things of life such as kayaking, golfing, bike riding, and long hikes. Looking forward to what the future has in store for Tweet and with new adventures.

CHAPTER 49

PRIDE COULD HAVE CRIPPLED MY LIFE

by Whitney Hartford
Creator, Mommin It Like A Boss
www.MomminItLikeABoss.com

My name is Whitney Hartford a/k/a Mommin It Like A Boss. I don't know about you, but for me 2021 was a whirlwind. I can't believe it's over. I will tell you this, my life has changed completely with some guidance and knowledge.

I was never a book reader. The funny thing is, I was an anti-book person. Not intentionally, I had a career that demanded me to read and prepare documents the majority of the time. The last thing I wanted to do was dive into a book. If I didn't read these two special books, I wouldn't have become a confident, strong boss mom that I am today.

I was going through a turbulent time in my life; I think we all were when Covid hit. During Covid, we had to relocate and we only had two months to find a house for a family of five with two animals. I found myself very discombobulated, exhausted and breaking down. We had a lot on our plate and, to be truthfully honest, I was looking for some direction. We had just had twins and, with everything going on, I felt like my ship was sinking. I prayed for guidance and I received it.

My mother introduced to me to my mentor, Genesis Hey Krick. She sent me a sweet gift in the mail to help me get on the right track and blessed me with her book *Shine On*, a 60-day devotional. Initially I thought, "How are the gifts she has given really going to help me?"

All I thought was it was more homework on top of the motivational coaching biz I started. That alone was a very detailed process on its own.

During my coaching sessions, I found myself looking at the book, then I would put it to the side and asked myself why wasn't I reading it? Reading was a goal I personally wanted to accomplish that year and I cannot deny in some way I was urging to get closer to God, so I opened the book and, to my surprise, it resonated with me and was simpler and more heartfelt than I expected. You see, the lady who was coaching me had gone through her own turbulent times. She taught me how to achieve a better mindset based around living each day with a purpose serving God through my journeys.

I cannot speak for everyone's interest in religion. I have my own personal experiences and as I started reading this book, I started to feel a personal change on how I worked through life's challenging seasons. Reading the devotional taught me how to find gratitude in chaos, that I was loved beyond measure for being myself, and how much I didn't realize it. There were bad habits I chose to work on breaking because I wasn't content with where I was in my life.

We are peer-pressured so much to follow society. I learned that I didn't need to follow the crowd to feel accepted and validated. Each day I read about how my mentor conquered her challenges and applied bible principles. At the end of each devotional, she would ask a couple of questions. This was a great way for me to reset and refocus. What especially stood out is when she was speaking about being your authentic self-unglamorized. I thought to myself how could this really work for me. I LOVE glam. I continued to read and sure enough just like her book there is so much more to me than meets the eye.

I think following the crowd can be easier than self-reflection and re-direction. I reflected and thought about how I could become better and happy for my family. Reading the devotional helped me gain the confidence to be the change I wanted for my family. Her book helped me start to live each day with more intention and I couldn't be more grateful that she shared her journey. I felt like my soul was being nourished each day and wanted to read more. I was fulfilled with my heart; the stress of real-life finances was still draining us. As a stay-at-home mom and mompreneur just starting a business can be hard, especially if you want to have minimum overhead.

So I picked another book to read around the same time! What better book than *The Total Money Makeover* written by Dave Ramsey? I hope that isn't too nerdy for you. So many people said what a great book it was and here I had one graciously given to me by an attorney I worked with. The book sat on my table waiting to be opened. I kid you not, the book wasn't opened for a year. That change I wanted to make for me and my family required me to suck it up and read a good book. I am still kicking myself in the butt for not opening it sooner. We could be a whole year more ahead than we are now. The point I am trying to make is that it's better late than never.

Ramsey's book showed me how much I didn't know and how I let pride get in my personal way to "living like no one else so I can live like no one else," Dave Ramsey says. If you have read the book or choose to read it, you will know what I am referencing.

My husband and I have been working really hard to follow the Dave Ramsey Debt Free plan and we already feel peace of mind knowing we are working towards a debt free future. We/I have learned how to get more creative with how we spend our money and more aware of what we spend our money on. Buying houses, credit cards, and having credit are all drilled into our heads as adults. If we teach our kids the value of having a debit-free life, they can live the life they want without the stress that most Americans live with today. I personally think a Dave Ramsey book should be given to every kid in high school. The book teaches people of all education levels how to achieve life debt free. Without the *Shine On Devotional* and *The Total Money Makeover*, I personally wouldn't have grown into a better person mentally and financially. Now we are a family with a financial plan, more faith than ever, and we are living our lives purposefully.

WHITNEY HARTFORD

Whitney Hartford is an ambitious mother and wife of three beautiful girls. She understands the struggles of being a single mother while working in the legal industry for five years. She worked as a legal assistant/paralegal and saw it as a great learning opportunity to broaden her skills. During this process, she was able to provide legal resources and consulting. She loved working in the field because it was a great educational experience.

She found herself going through In vitro fertilization (IVF). It can be an exhausting physical and emotional process. Working full time, she found herself pregnant with twins after her second IVF cycle. She worked full time and worked out until she delivered her twin girls. This has driven her to pursue passions which were inspired by going through the IVF process in 2019, having a love for fitness and fashion, while she cares for her toddler twin girls and 10-year-old.

She uses fitness to strengthen her weaknesses, mind, and body. She uses fashion to express her creativity, saves the environment, and thrifts like a boss which has led to her opening her online store Bangin Vintage! She shares her life experiences as an influencer and the creator of Mommin It Like A Boss to inspire her peers and other women so they can Mom It Like A Boss. As a mompreneur, she is here to empower and inspire you to find comfort in your chaos. As a mompreneur, she is here to empower and inspire you to find comfort in your chaos.

Connect with Whitney here: www.MomminItLikeABoss.com

CHAPTER 50

JESUS, MARY (WELL, ESTHER) AND JOSEPH

by Whitnie Wiley
Founder & Chief Evolution Officer, Shifting Into Action
https://shiftingintoaction.now.site

The ultimate love story.

Yes, the *Bible* is, first and foremost, a love story.

It's also life's instruction manual. Most people generally see the instruction part. They are focused on what God says they can do, or what they cannot do. Clearly, there are a lot of things we should not do, and the *Bible* lays them out. However, the principles within are beyond a list of rules, or the dos and don'ts.

It's about God's love for us, as well as what our lives can become when we love Him in return. The *Bible* teaches how we can transform into the image and likeness of the Creator, allowing the rules to fade into the background and become a way of life.

Until I read the *Bible*, I wasn't aware that God was wooing me to live my best life by living according to His will. I was only tangentially knowledgeable about the contents, and what little I knew, wasn't appealing.

I'd heard it said, "Christians are the only *Bible* some people read." If reading the *Bible* would make me like some of the "Christians" I'd met, I needed a new goal.

My early exposure to Christians and some, even to this day, is antithetical to my understanding of God's Word. We are not called to hate people. Their behaviors, yes, but people no. The *Bible* expresses God's desire for forgiveness, justice, mercy, grace—and most importantly—love.

There are hundreds of stories in the *Bible*, and while not all are pleasant, the underlying message is simply this—God loves His creation, particularly humankind. That love drove Him to give His only son, Jesus, to pay for our sins so that we would have everlasting life—a life with Him.

When I put God first and align my desires with His will, He gives me the desires of my heart, working all things of life out, for my good. Does that mean I get everything I want? No. But I get what's "for my good," or in other words, what is best in the grander picture I may not yet know.

God makes it clear—I have free will. My actions have consequences. My choices impact and influence other people's choices and consequences, as do theirs on me. God is working all these seemingly random acts and choices out for my good, and for those who love Him. The first and most important choice I make with my free will—is to love Him.

There are three Biblical characters who have significantly impacted how I live my life: Jesus, Esther, and Joseph, not the father of Jesus, but Joseph of the amazing technicolor dreamcoat.

Jesus is Mary and Joseph's son. It's a complicated concept, but it boils down to this. Mary was a virgin engaged to marry Joseph, the carpenter, not the technicolor dreamcoat Joseph. An angel appeared telling her despite never having had relations with a man, including Joseph, she would deliver God's son and name him Jesus.

Jesus was delivered by a human and raised by a human to live the life of a human, even though he was God in the flesh. This matters because he needed to live the human experience before fulfilling his purpose— to die for humankind and pay humanity's sin debt. God's perfection prevents him from being near sin, and humanity's punishment for sin is death. God banished Adam and Eve from the Garden of Eden when they revealed their disobedience after eating from the tree of knowledge of good and evil. That act resulted in the continual decay of humanity through subsequent generations. While death was not immediate, death was imminent, as God initially intended us to live forever.

God created a plan to reconcile me to Him. Jesus is that plan. God's love for me is so deep that He allows me to make the choice that Adam and Eve stole when they sinned. God doesn't require that I live a perfect life. However, by not choosing Him, I live a life that is devoid of fellowship with Him, which is living a life in hell.

That was my life before the *Bible*. I lived a selfish life focused on immediate gratification instead of being guided by my life's purpose—to glorify God. I didn't know better, so I couldn't do better, but that all changed.

My transformation started during an encounter with God, leading me to the church. In my first meeting with the Pastor, I cried and poured out my heart, my pain. I knew I needed to live differently. I had this deep desire to know God—something I hadn't known was even possible. I knew *of* God and had thought that was enough. I wanted to read the *Bible* but couldn't, thinking it was complex and tedious, but the reality, I wasn't ready.

Any reading would have been merely an academic exercise rather than the life-changing transformation I needed. So, Pastor suggested I not read the *Bible* cover to cover but start in the New Testament. That's where I learned about God's love for me.

Comprehending God's love and His plan became a passion. By the time I got to Genesis, I was hooked and able to glide through the challenging passages that had previously halted my progress. Since then, I've read the *Bible* several times, with different approaches, and various understanding because I'm not the same person.

It wasn't simply reading the book, but *taking action* because of the book that changed my life and prepared me to survive and thrive through the darkest days of my life. I was going to church regularly, involved with ministry, making connections, and living a life filled with forgiveness and grace—for others and myself. In addition to the *Bible*, *The Purpose Driven Life* by Rick Warren helped me connect to God and why I'm here. Being aligned with my purpose allowed me to move through life when death was pervasive.

After my son died in 2005, my faith in God's plan and commitment to my life's purpose saw me through. The same faith and commitment continue to guide me to this day. I kept reading my *Bible* to understand how to live with indescribable pain. It helped me when I couldn't pray or muster the strength to go to church.

Reading the *Bible* hasn't made my life perfect, but it's helped me understand how to flow with life in a way I hadn't before. Do I have all the answers? No.

Joseph's story and how he navigated his life amidst deep sorrow and incredible challenges shed light on how I could too live my life for God's glory.

Joseph's ten brothers, jealous because he was their father's favorite son, mistreated him. They planned to kill him, but eventually they sold him to merchants who took him to Egypt. While in Egypt, he was jailed because of false accusations for refusing to sleep with his boss's wife in order to remain clean before God. Despite his circumstances, he received God's favor. After years in slavery and being a prisoner, Joseph's ability to interpret dreams came to the Pharoah's attention. He was able to interpret Pharoah's dreams when no one else could. Pharoah rewarded Joseph by making him his second in command.

At some point, Joseph's brothers seek grain in Egypt. Pharoah's dreams told Joseph how the world would survive the famine by storing crops during the prosperous years. As predicted in the dreams Joseph shared with his brothers as a kid, they bowed down to him, begging for his mercy to provide food for their family.

Joseph's story is a perfect example of how, although some mean to do evil, God uses it in our lives for good—if we trust Him.

Esther's story reiterates how God plants us where we are meant to be for His purposes. Esther, a Jew, was the wife of Persia's King Xerxes. She replaced Queen Vashti after the king exiled her for disobeying his orders. One of the King's servants, Haman, tricked him into adopting laws to exterminate the Jews, which Esther learned from her uncle Mordecai, Haman's enemy.

Mordecai convinced Esther to risk death and ask the King for a reprieve for her people. He reminded her that it was likely she was queen for such a situation as they were in. With a well-thought-out plan, she approached the King, without permission, which could have meant death. She was granted entry and asked her husband for a favor. Esther, having no authority to change the law, convinced King Xerxes to issue new laws permitting Jews to defend themselves.

When you know someone loves you, and everything they do is for your best and highest good, it changes you. That's what reading the *Bible* and understanding God's Word has done for me. Regardless of the messes I've made in my life, He's always with me. As I've learned to trust and turn to Him, whether I see it happening or not, I know because of His love for me and I love Him, He is working all things out for my good.

WHITNIE WILEY

After her son's death and finding it difficult to say out loud much of what she was experiencing, Whitnie Wiley began her journey as a speaker and author by chronicling her grief.

Since those painful early days, Whitnie has shared her thoughts on leadership and career management with hundreds of thousands of readers around the world as the author for the *Lead the Way* column in the Association of Corporate Counsel's *Docket* magazine and contributor to multiple bestselling books, including *The Fearless Entrepreneurs*, *Women Who Empower* and several *1 Habit* titles. She encourages her readers to develop self-awareness and use their values and priorities to pave their path to enjoying their careers, better leadership, and improved teamwork.

As an in-demand coach and speaker, Whitnie shares wisdom from her life experiences with grace, humility, and humor to drive change in today's business world by helping professional women transition to the career of their dreams.

Whitnie is Jesuit trained in organizations and leadership with bachelor's and master's degrees from the University of San Francisco and St. Joseph's University, respectively, and a Juris Doctor from Alliant International University's San Francisco Law School. She has certifications as a trainer and coach specializing in career management and transitions.

You can reach her at: Whitnie@ShiftingIntoAction.com or 916.304.4742.

Additionally, you can find Whitnie on LinkedIn http://www.linkedin.com/in/whitniewiley and in her Facebook group www.faccbook.com/groups/dreamjobcareerconnection.

AFTERWORD

It is our sincere hope that these stories have not only caused you to think, but to ACT! As you read through the transformations, you have seen the authors experience many breakthroughs. They made a decision to uplevel their lives. The common thread through all of our stories is that we chose not to stay stuck and made a "decision" to transform our lives through the books we've read.

May today be the day you are inspired to choose to create the life you deserve, be courageous enough to act, and surround yourself with inspirational and motivational people who want you to win.

Today is the perfect day to Take Action!

If any of these stories resonated with you, please connect with the authors. They are here to help you create the life you truly want to live.

With Love,

Lynda Sunshine West and Sally Larkin Green

COMPLETE LIST OF ALL BOOKS MENTIONED

Book Title	Author Name	Chapter	Book I Read Author
1 Habit for Entrepreneurial Success	Steve Samblis, Forbes Riley	2	Sally Larkin Green
5 am Club (The)	Robin Sharma	8	Bryan Allen-Smith
Acres of Diamonds	Russell Conwell	22	Kim Kelley Thompson
Adventures of the Soul	James Van Praagh	17	Jaymie Hale
Answer is Energy (The)	Jarrad Hewett	21	Kim Jacobs Martin
Artist's Way (The)	Julia Cameron	24	Kristy Boyd Johlson
Autobiography of a Yogi	Paramahansa Yogananda	28	Lorrel Elian
Best Gluten-Free Cookbook (The)	Donna Washburn, Heather Butt	48	Tweet Larkin
Bible (The)		7	Bridgetti Lim Banda
Bible (The)		40	Romy Faith Ganser
Bible (The)		50	Whitnie Wiley
Breaking the Habit of Being Yourself	Joe Dispenza	39	Rita Farruggia
Building a Story Brand	Donald Miller	44	Sherri Leopold
Caste	Isabel Wilkerson	16	Greer McVay
Checklist Manifesto (The)	Atul Gawande	37	Prophetess Nalo Thomas
Conversations With God	Neale Donald Walsch	35	Nancy Lockhart
Dare to Lead	Brené Brown	15	Farah Ismail
Daring Greatly	Brené Brown	9	Cathy Derksen
Do It Afraid	Joyce Meyer	6	Becky Musbrucker

Book Title	Author Name	Chapter	Book I Read Author
E-Squared	Pam Grout	13	Debbie Morton
Energy Speaks	Lee Harris	31	Mary Jackson
Four Agreements (The)	Don Miguel Ruiz, Janet Mills	5	Asma Yousif
Four Agreements (The)	Don Miguel Ruiz, Janet Mills	18	Jennifer Jerald
Four Agreements (The)	Don Miguel Ruiz, Janet Mills	43	Shanna Lee Moore
Girl, Stop Apologizing	Rachel Hollis	29	Lynnette LaRoche
Greatest Salesman in the World (The)	Og Mandino	12	David Blackford
Greatest Salesman in the World (The)	Og Mandino	22	Kim Kelley Thompson
Harriet Tubman: Conductor on the Underground Railroad	Ann Petry	19	Julie Brown
Ho'oponopono: The Hawaiian Forgiveness Ritual	Ulrich Emil Duprée	25	Krysten Maracle
How to Win Friends and Influence People	Dale Carnegie	47	Terry Shepherd
Lies My Doctor Told Me	Dr. Ken Berry	36	Paige Davidson
Master Key System (The)	Charles F. Haanel	2	Sally Larkin Green
Math Textbook		23	Kohila Sivas
Miracle Morning (The)	Hal Elrod, Robert Kiyosaki	14	Evan Trad
My Life with Karma	Travis Sackett	46	Teresa Cundiff
Oh, the Places You'll Go!	Dr. Seuss	33	Melodie Donovan
Originals: How Non-Conformists Move the World	Adam Grant, Sheryl Sandberg	30	Maria E De Lira
Outwitting the Devil	Napoleon Hill	34	Mistie Layne

Book Title	Author Name	Chapter	Book I Read Author
Power vs. Force	David R. Hawkins	38	Rebecca Norrigton
Pushing Up People	Art Williams	41	Sabrina Protic
Richest Man in Babylon (The)	George S. Clason	12	David Blackford
Secret (The)	Rhonda Byrne	13	Debbie Morton
Self-Bullying: What To Do When the Bully Is YOU	Sherri Leopold	11	Dara Bose
Shack (The)	William Paul Young	27	Legend Thurman
Success Principles (The)	Jack Canfield	1	Lynda Sunshine West
Sun Does Shine (The)	Anthony Ray Hinton, Lara Love Hardin	10	Christina Sorensen
Surrender Experiment (The)	Michael A. Singer	4	Annie Rettic
Think and Grow Rich	Napoleon Hill	42	Sandra Barker-McIntosh
Total Money Makeover	Dave Ramsey	49	Whitney Hartford
What the Bleep Do We Know!?	William Arntz	26	Latara Dragoo
Who Moved My Cheese?	Dr. Spencer Johnson, Kenneth Blanchard	45	Sohaila Handelsman
Who's In Your Room	Ivan R. Misner, Ph.D., Stewart Emery L.H.D., and Rick Sapi	3	Alice Palum
Women With Attention Deficit Disorder	Sari Solden	20	Julie Donelson
Wrinkle in Time (A)	Madeleine L'Engle	24	Kristy Boyd Johlson
You Can If You Think You Can	Norman Vincent Peale	32	Melissa Walsh